WHO KILLED MR DRUM?

WHO KILLED MR DRUM?

BY FRASER GRACE AND SYLVESTER STEIN

A TRUE STORY BASED ON THE BOOK BY **SYLVESTER STEIN**

OBERON BOOKS
LONDON

First published in this adaptation in 2005 by Oberon Books Ltd
521 Caledonian Road, London N7 9RH
Tel: 020 7607 3637 / Fax: 020 7607 3629
e-mail: oberon.books@btinternet.com
www.oberonbooks.com

A catalogue record for this book is available from the British
Library.

ISBN: 1 84002 610 3

Cover photograph by Jurgen Schadeburg

Printed in Great Britain by Antony Rowe Ltd, Chippenham.

Die wit man moet altyd baas wees.

The white man must always remain boss.

JG Strijdom, Prime Minister, S A, 1954–8

Under apartheid, a black man lived a shadowy life between legality and illegality, between openness and concealment. To be a black man in South Africa meant not to trust anything…

Nelson Mandela, *Long Walk to Freedom*

The truth is clear; it is heard all the time…echoing inside our ears, reverberating within the hard-boned skull, full of foreboding. The reverberations, if you succumb to them, can bring madness or death.

Hilda Bernstein, *The World That Was Ours*

Ay me. That was the Sophiatown that was.

Can Themba, *Requiem for Sophiatown*

Acknowledgements

The authors would like to offer heartfelt thanks to all those who helped in the research and writing of this play.

The story itself demanded that a play be written, but it would not have been possible without the support of Andrew Fishwick and Sarah Trahearn at Treatment Theatre, and in particular Paul Robinson's determination, dramaturgy, and vision. We would also especially like to thank Jurgen Schadeburg, whose photographs document so beautifully the period in which the play is set, and Claudia, his wife.

Extracts from Can Themba's obituary for *Mr Drum, Henry Nxumalo*, and from *Crespuscle* and *The Will to Die*, are used by kind permission, while inspiration was also drawn from the writings of Ezekiel Mphahlele, Bloke Modisane, Todd Matshikiza, Casey Motsisi and Arthur Maimane; the last of whom exists in spirit in these pages.

Characters
(in order of speaking)

SERGEANT BEZUIDENHOUT
Afrikaans cop

SYL STEIN
White, Jewish South African, Drum's recently appointed editor

CAN THEMBA
Assistant Editor, the fast-living, womanising,
'Shakespeare of the Shebeens'

HENRY NXUMALO
Chief Reporter. Hard-drinking gambler and
former Sports Reporter

BOB GOSANI
Photographer. Late teens, slim and lithe

BLOKE MODISANE
The 'debonair' society correspondent and lover of fine living

CASEY MOTSISI
Sports Reporter, and the gang's bookie

DOLLY RATHEBE
Amply proportioned African beauty, singer and cover-girl

TODD MATSHIKIZA
Laid-back music writer, jazz musician and composer

LIZZIE HUTCHINSON
Pale-skinned English beauty

ZEKE MPHAHLELE
Educated, sober-minded, lover of literature, a radical

MOETSIE
African cop

Other roles played by cast:

Tsotsis (gangsters), other cops

Who Killed Mr Drum? was first produced by Treatment Theatre at The Riverside Studios on 1 September 2005. The cast, in order of speaking, was as follows:

SERGEANT BEZUIDENHOUT, Jon Cartwright

SYLVESTER STEIN, Stephen Billington

CAN THEMBA, Sello Maake Ka-Ncube

HENRY NXUMALO, Wale Ojo

BOB, Wela Frasier

BLOKE, Israel Aduramo

CASEY, Marcel McCalla

DOLLY, Andi Osho

TODD / TSOTSI, Emmanuel Ighodaro

LIZZIE, Georgina Sutcliffe

ZEKE, Lucian Msamati

MOETSIE / TSOTSI, Ayodeji Aloba

Director Paul Robinson

Creative Producer Andrew Fishwick

Designer Francisco Rodriguez-Weil

Lighting Designer Ben Ormerod

Sound Designer Paul Groothuis

Composer Juwon Ogungbe

Image Designer Andrew Savage

Movement Directors Bernadette Iglich, Andile Sotiya

Fight Director Terry King

Dialect Coach Sally Hague

Casting Director Sam Jones

Assistant Producer Sarah Trahearn

1

Lights up on a patch of street, odd sheets of newspaper lying around. Newspapers also cover a body. The body, which lies on its back, one arm tucked under, has shed a shoe, which lies close by.

CAN sits nearby, very ruffled suit, a blood-stained hat in his hands.

Seeing SYL approach stage right, CAN stands. As he does so, Bezuidenhout (BEZ) a cop, enters stage left.

Bez I put the body under cover Meneer. Keep off the sun.

SYL nods in appreciation.

Syl Thank you.

They stare at the body. BEZ shakes his head.

Bez Blerry kaffirs hey? Always taking a man from his rest. The boy here gave you as the employer. For identifying.

Syl Can? What happened?

CAN flaps his arms helplessly. BEZ moves toward the body.

Bez Every night some black-on-black murder. Always shouting and fighting – especially at New Year's. Parties, illegal drink. Whores and gangsters. So many knives in the district.

He shakes his head.

Damn shame for this kaffir though. You will confirm the identity, ja?

SYL nods. BEZ removes one of the sheets, revealing HENRY's upper body. CAN looks away, he's already seen it.

Syl It's Henry. Henry Nxumalo. Christ.

(*Turning away.*) Jesus Christ, Can. I mean Jesus bloody Christ, man!!

Can It's alright, boss. It's OK.

Syl Henry though!! Jesus!

Can (*Acknowledging the awfulness.*) Ja. Ja…

Pause. CAN passes HENRY's hat to SYL. SYL handles it reverently, looking at it. After a while a thought is triggered.

Syl Purse. Did you find that? Sergeant, what happened to this man's purse?

Bez Investigations are confidential, meneer. Not for the ears of this naytiff.

Syl For godsake, this is my Assistant Editor, Can Themba.

Bez What, this kaffir?

Beat. SYL bites his lip, and resorts to calling on a racial connection.

Syl Look, you dragged me out of bed on a public holiday. I'd appreciate some help.

Beat. This is a point won by BEZ – or at least a draw – and he gives way.

Bez The boy was robbed. He resisted. Or some naytiff felt like killing. Another comes after, takes the purse and runs. Send Jim here to the station tomorrow – maybe he can bring you a message…

Can And that's it? That's all you know?

Bez Hey, less of your cheek now, alright. You are on the scene pretty quick yourself…

Can I was called out here…!

10

Bez Hou jou fockin bek kaffir! Didn't I just warn you!?...
You can make a blerry suspect too! You raise your voice
to me, (*Hand on his stick.*) I'll donner you, ja!

Syl Alright, Sergeant, for Christsake!!!

Can's upset. We both are. Henry was our friend.

Bez Robbing. That is the motive. Or some blerry tsotsi
with a knife to try. Later we can prove it.

Syl Can?

Beat.

Can I don't know, man. Maybe he was working.

Beat.

Something he was talking about. You heard of Black
Velvet? Where the police pick up a black girl –

Bez (*Cutting him off.*) Come to the station, Meneer, that is
the best. Sign in the book. Then this body can go to the
family. Naytiffs bury quick, this time of year.

Syl My God, Henry's family. Jesus!

*Beat. BEZ picks up a shoe, lying a way off. He strolls around
the crime scene.*

Bez Your boetie was brave, meneer. Kicks his attacker, for
the shoe to come off. Cut repeatedly – to the face, chest,
belly, also the hands. That is what makes the blood here.
Break the head with a sjambok – or the brick from this
rubble – look, you see? – then with the knife, for killing.
The way they do it in the bush.

Separate Development – that is what is coming, thank
God. Capeys, kaffirs, coolies... Each man a district to
his kind. My god, Meneer! This place will be full of you
Englisch!

Too late for this Henry, ja.

BEZ tosses the rock and the shoe down, close to the body, and turns to exit. CAN bridles. SYL restrains him.

Syl No. No! For godsake… (I can't lose you as well…)

Bez (*Turning, to SYL.*) Naturelle Themba, ja? You keep this boy out of my district. Tell him. He will get himself a helluva beating.

BEZ exits. CAN shakes himself free. Pause.

Can I need a drink. Wash that damn fly out of my mouth. Come on, man.

CAN's exit is halted by SYL who lingers, looking at HENRY's body.

Syl We'll get the bastard who did this. If we do nothing else, we do this.

Can (*Scoffing, despondent.*) Sure.

CAN exits. SYL lingers, picking something small from the dust near HENRY. He examines it, pockets it, and exits, leaving us alone with the body.

Light change. HENRY appears before us.

Henry Johannesburg, New Year's Day. First of the first, 1957. The streets of Sophiatown are humming with a new tune today, a tune that trips from the lips of every native girl and native boy, all across the city.

He stares at the patch. He puts on his hat, bends down, picks up two small rocks, strikes them gently together.

And the name of that tune? Why, you heard it….

He looks out.

Who killed Mr Drum?

The grin spreads across his face again, as township music kicks in. The scene change whirls into action…

2

A chattering typewriter.

Lights up on Drum Magazine's first floor office, Johannesburg.

It is the morning of Friday, 28 December 1956.

Upstage, a glass door to the editor's office, in which SYL can be glimpsed.

Further doors lead to the exit/stairs, and to a small dark room.

A high window, upstage looks onto the street.

Inside the newsroom, DOLLY sits perched on a desk, legs seductively crossed, polishing her nails. BLOKE peers out of the window.

BOB sits close by reading a pile of letters; opening the envelopes, laughing at the contents.

Bob O man, that is just the biscuit!

Hey Casey, you read this one?

Bloke Hey Bobby, where's your noblesse oblige? Read the letters to the lady to whom these missives are addressed.

Bob Me? Read to Dolly?

Casey Man's right, man.

Dolly Yes, you can read 'em Bobby, I'll listen caareful.

Bob (*Gulping, not too fluently.*) Dear Dolly Heartbreak – I am a one hundred per cent African woman, but I got a wonderful Coloured boyfriend. He gets me presents all the time! He also got me a lot pregnant, and my husband expects it's going to be black, like him. The truth is coming out soon, Dolly, I don't think I can hold it in much longer.

Bloke (*Laughing, taking the letter.*) Please give me advices Dolly – yours faithfully, Distraught of Orlando.

Casey Man, I love that faithfully…

Dolly You boys are too cruel.

She takes letter, passes it back to BOB. CASEY is back to his typing.

Bob So, what do you want Dolly? You want to answer just for once, or d'you want us to do it?

Dolly You are on your own boys. I gotta go down to Ah Sings records, see if I'm a hot property yet. You tell that Can Themba I came like he said, only he wasn't here. Alright?

Bloke (*Taking letter.*) Never mind Bob, looks like a job for we dedicated newspapermen…

Phone rings – all look at it.

Casey Bloke – pull finger – what the hang does Mr Bailey pay you for?!

Bloke And you man? I'm doing Dolly here.

Casey Bob can do Dolly. She's easy enough.

Beat.

Dolly What?

Casey Just, get the damn phone man.

Dolly Why don't you try talking nicely, Casey?

Mister Modisane sir, would you mind inclining your ear to the telephone, for a moment?

Bloke For you it would be a pleasure, mademoiselle.

14

(*Phone.*) Drum Magazine?

He listens briefly, recoils with a grimace, holding the receiver away from his ear.

Dolly Trouble comes, I go. (*Vamp.*) Bye boys...

All (*Helpless.*) Bye Dolly...

Bloke (*Phone.*) I'm sorry missis, I have to cut you off now.

He puts the phone down, and sighs.

Bibi again, man. Can Themba is in serious trouble with that fraulein. Takes me a whole year to annoy two women. He gets it done in a week!

Casey That's Canadoce.

CASEY snatches paper from the typewriter.

OK here it is. The streets of Sophiatown are being bulldozed for the Resettlement Program. We Drum boys must respond.

Bob That's right, man.

Bloke No no not us man. The readers. Drum magazine calls all who care about Sophiatown, to contemplate the awfulness of the present situation. Which of our beloved streets might survive the bulldozers this year? We must all stick together.

Casey Right. So. We got, two-to-one Good Street. Four-to-one Miller street. Five-to-one Gold Street, Gibson Street and Main Road.

Bloke Woah – do you give Good Street more chance to survive than Miller Street?

Casey Yes I do – The Odin Cinema is in Good Street.

Bob He is right, man. People like the movies.

Bloke Man, there's shebeens every four yards in Miller
Street. Does a shebeen mean nothing to you boys?

Bob Shebeen means drinks, man. Pin-ups. Barberton.
Specially at New Years.

Bloke And what else, beside liquor?

Casey Ladies, man. And if Can's around, a lot of
intellectual conversation.

Bob And even more ladies…

Casey / Bob …like Dolleeee!

Bloke Boys boys boys – you have got to think a little!
Where there's a shebeen, there's money for the police
– bribes and so forth. It don't matter to them, they got
their whites-only cinemas, they are bound to take Good
Street first.

Casey I'm happy. What you say, Bob? Miller at twos…
Good at threes?

Bob Hold up Casey. You never said Gerty Street.

Casey Gerty Street – are you serious?

*Enter HENRY, carrying an armful of newspapers. He hangs
his hat on a hook.*

Henry Gerty Street. Now who in the hang is talking about
Gerty Street?

Casey Hey, Hen, how's it going man!

Henry 'Hen'? Hey, Hen?

Casey (*Adjusting status.*) Henry. Captain. How goes it? You
pass Dolly on the stair?

Henry O I stood aside for miss Dolly. No room for two
when Dolly's coming at you.

It goes good, Kid. Thank you.

Bloke Mister Henry Nxumalo, undercover journalist extraordinaire. Do we know you?

Bob Wow Mr Drum's in all those papers?

Henry Mr Drum does get a mention…

Casey (*Consulting newspaper.*) – page two, page four, page six and page seven – the appalling treatment dealt out to natives in jail, as first reported in that erstwhile jazz rag, Drum Magazine.' Tremendous, man.

Bloke Yee-sus!

Bob Golden City Post, Jo'burg star – it's true, you're a legend, Uncle Henry.

Henry As I will say in my acceptance speech,
Drum magazine is a team effort. We are a team of thoroughbred news giants.

Still no Canadoce, hey.

Bloke Not yet man.

Henry How about old Sylvester? He around?

Casey On the telephone. All morning so far. Boss is busy, weather's fine and the coast is clear.

Phone rings. Again all watch it.

Henry We not answering the telephone today?

Bob Not me, man. That's Bibi.

Henry Can's woman. Bibi?

Bloke She's missing Can too.

Casey Want me to get it Henry? Could be business.

Henry Sure man. Strike while we're hot.

Casey (*Phone.*) Drum Magazine, Casey 'the Kid Motsisi' deputising for Mr Henry Nxumalo, the Famous Mr

Drum… O hello Bibi, no, Iss Casey here, what can I do for you girl…

Henry Say, Bloke. Take a look out of the window. Is there a man standing on the corner out there?

BLOKE crosses to window, stretching to see.

Casey (*Phone.*) Yeah. No. No no no. Absol – Of course…

Bloke Yeah, what's up Henry?

Henry Bus comes and goes, he's still stood there.

Casey (*Phone.*) No I swear, girl, we didn't see Can at all this week…

Bloke That oukie in the sports coat? He's been there all morning, man.

Casey (*Phone.*) I will, I will pass that on to him… Yes I will.

Bob (*Standing on a stool.*) Tweed jacket? Looks like Special Branch, to me.

Bloke Special Branch has a mackintosh, man. That's Secret Service. You got a tail Henry?

Casey (*Phone.*) …O hey, you wouldn't do that, Bibi, would you…

Bob (*Alarmed.*) A tail?

Henry No, no, you said it man. He's been there all morning. Waiting for Dolly to leave, so he can walk her home.

Bloke He could be after any of us Braves, this could be serious.

Casey (*Phone.*) I won't forget, Bibi, I promise…

Henry You'll be alright, Bloke – just tone down your art reviews.

Casey (*Phone.*) I'll tell him. I will. Bye now.

Phone down. CASEY sighs, heavily.

Bibi thinks Can's cheating on her again…

Bloke Why does Can always go for those thinking women…?

Henry (*Spotting CAN at the door, shaking his head.*) O ay yaiiy and here he is, seems you are the walking dead, Can Themba.

Casey Ja, you've got two women on your tail today man.

Enter CAN looking dishevelled.

Can Easy boys. I need some sensitivity here. My head's aching with the pressure of life. Two women?

Bloke You just missed Dolly.

Can Hang, I did?

Henry If you've got a sore head my friend, that's Barberton, not Bibi …

Casey Hey Can, hoozit, man.

Can Hoozit kid. Boys. Hey Hen, hoozit with you Bru?

HENRY and CAN embrace.

They let you out of jail already? Why'd they do that?

Henry You heard about that?

Can You are a star in the stratosphere, Henry.

Henry Barberton again. You're always seeing stars.

Can Not those kind of stars. Not a drop of Barberton has touched my lips since last weekend.

Bob That's why you look so rough, man – no drink!

Casey Where've you bin man. Syl's going crazy you not turning up.

Can O, I've just been hanging out at my residence, the 'House of Truth' – locked in solitary contemplation of the heavens. A man reaches a time in his life – Henry will back me on this – when he has no need for strong drink. When is that time? When he finds something for which it is worth staying sober. For Henry here, it is the journalistic life. For me, it is…other things. Of which freedom is the greatest. Don't you smile Casey. It could happen to you one day.

Casey No drink? If you see that coming, you warn me boys.

Henry The House of Truth, that what you call your place now?

Can The House of Truth, where no word is spoken, and nothing sought but the truth and the freedom to enjoy that truth. In the words of Mister Charles Dickens, I ask only to be free as the butterfly is free. Mankind will surely not deny, what it concedes to the butterfly.

So. What's up boys?

Casey Oh we just organising us a little flutter on the resettlement.

Bloke Now where have we got to on that streetstake, Casey?

Bob Gerty Street…

Casey No no, not Gerty Street.

Bob Why not, man?

Casey You can't have Gerty Street, Bob.

Bob My ma lives on Gerty Street!

Casey The odds are too long man. She's only two streets from where the bulldozers were in Toby Street a month back.

Bob It doesn't always work that way. White people are not logical. Tell him Henry. Ma Bob says she's staying in her house, whatever the Nats do. They can demolish the whole of Soph'town she is not going to move one lonely inch.

Casey Ma-Bob may stay fixed till the end of time Bobby, her walls are leaving tomorrow...

Henry Does Ma-Bob have a Permission-to-Remain stamp in her Pass yet, Bobby?

Bob I don't think so. They won't give her one. You think that's it for her?

Henry What do you say, Mr Themba? How do things looks from that House of Truth of yours, where no word is spoken but the truth...

Can Well let me see. (*To BOB, pronouncing judgement.*) Your ma lives in Gerty Street, and she doesn't have her permission to stay?

Did someone call me the walking dead just now?

Bloke O man, the Truth can be cruel...

HENRY pulls out his pipe and loads it.

Casey I can't do nothing for Gerty Street, Bob. She'd be fifty-to-one at least, thass a waste of everyone's time.

Bob Hang Casey, you gotta let us have it.

Henry I'll take it.

Beat.

Can Henry? Henry Nxumalo puts money on Gerty street? Come on Henry...

Henry Why not. The odds are good. You say fifty-to-one Casey?

Pause. CASEY is speechless, he looks from CAN to HENRY and back.

Can Take it Casey.

Casey But…

Can If a man goes crazy, that's no reason not to take his money. In fact, I'd say it was a duty…

Bloke Wait just a mo there, man. You got a inside track on this, Henry?

Henry Inside track on relocation. What would that be Bloke? Which bulldozer is off his oats today? Which cop's breathing heavy in the paddock?

Casey Man's right, it's slum clearance we're talking here, not the July fucking handicap.

Henry In fact, why don't we make it – Five pounds.

Casey Five pounds…?!!!

Bloke Shi-iit man, you on white wages now?

Henry No man. Boss-man Bailey gave me a bonus, that's all. For the Jail story.

Bloke Jim Bailey gave you a bonus?

Casey (*To CAN.*) Why does he get a bonus?

Can He earned it, I guess. All this trailblazing copy he serves up.

Casey What? A couple of nights in jail and a little beating? I get that every weekend, I don't get a bonus!

Henry I don't say I'm a 'Shakespeare of the Shebeens' like you, but it's a cut above the usual nonsense.

Can You may be right, Hen. My guess boys, is Mr Drum's already working on a brand new exposé. You going to tell us what it is?

Casey Ja? Exposé of what, man?

Pause – HENRY is not saying.

Can Bob?

Bob You know Uncle Henry. It's all undercover with him.

Beat.

Can You know what? I'm disappointed in you boys. I'm afraid this Mr Drum of ours is going to give Drum Magazine a very, very bad name round here.

Casey What? Come on man, we are making the best stir ever because of Henry. That's how he gets the damn raise.

Can Well now, I know for a fact Henry missed the biggest story in town this month.

Henry And what would that be Bru. You not drinking any more?

Can I'm talking hot and hard news. I'm talking the further, nocturnal adventures, of Drum Magazine's true undercovers agent... I give you, Canadoce Amitikula von Themba. Master of Romance. And gentleman about the town.

Henry There you go, Bloke. Fiction has a place after all.

Casey Ooooh man – that's it! You bin with a woman all week! No wonder Bibi gone crazy!!

Bloke So tell us amigo, who was this Queen of Sheeba?

Casey This that new Shona girl from Braamfontein?

Bob Peggy Pendula? Who man?

Can This lady's none of that kind, Bob. Another tribe entirely, if I may say so.

Bloke Sesutu? Xhosa?

Can Don't think Nguni at all, Bloke.

Casey Not Capey?!

Can Not Indian nor Chinese. This lady is what you might call, untouched by the orient…that is, till I got her hooked…

Bloke Untouched by… O my gots! Ay, ja jaaiy! That only leaves…

Casey Jeezus man!

Can Brand new import!

Casey English!

Bloke O my god! Get that word down, Bob – English, Engelse, Anglaise!

Can Ssssh, not a word, Modisane! Sylvester may hear. We don't want Mr Editor knowing all my seditious business. Not yet anyhow.

Casey O my gots!

Bloke Sir, you are in trouble again! You never heard of the Immorality Act?! That Special Branch swine-hound was for you, man!

Can Special Branch?

Henry Nothing, man.

Casey Wow – you hear that Henry, ol' Can got Silverfish last night!

Henry 'Silverfish'?

WHO KILLED MR DRUM?

Can That's not a real nice term Casey. My Lizzie, she's just a nice wasp-waisted, broad-minded girl from London, England.

Bloke (*Shaking his head.*) O my godfathers.

Casey Nice curves, hey?

Can Artist's dream.

Henry So, would that be Picasso, hey Bru?

Can I'd say, more on the Botticelli principle, Hen. Soft skin, classic nose, delicious big eyes looking deep into yours, and smooth long golden hair going all the way down…

Bob O my God. Blondie!

Henry (*Laughing.*) Out with your secret Can Themba. What is it you do for those white ladies?

Can No secret, Hen, just genius.

Bloke Is this that Lizzie Hutchinson we saw you flirting with at the party last week? That pale skin, English Lizzie? Funny, I heard she had a husband.

Can It's true. She might be…slightly married.

Bloke I tell you Henry, I have seen this Liz-girl dance the kwela like a black ladeeee…

BLOKE perhaps dances a step or two of kwela.

Can There was a hush falls on the house, when I showed her round to Little Heaven last night...

Bob What?! You gone public with her?!!

Casey Black man goes crazy in Sof'town!

Henry So that's where you were this week, hey Bru. Putting this poor white woman to all kinds of inconvenience…

25

Casey I can imagine what followed for sure, hey Can, how the night ended for you two. Silverfish!

Bob (*Starts to get carried away.*) Sil-ver-fiiiissh!

Bloke Ol' Bibi is going to hear about this for sure! That's it! She did already! 'I am SO humiliated, Can Themba, you cheated on me with a white laydeee!!!'

Laughter, which is stolen by SYL, entering, which all notice just in time except BOB.

Bob (*Continuing.*) Sil-ver-fiiiissh!

Syl Ah Henry you're here. Bob.

Bob How do you do, Mr Stein.

Syl Good, thanks. O, and Canadoce. Glad you could join us.

Beat.

Can I was just telling the boys here I had to go down to the Pass Office this morning. Tug my hair out, get my permission stamp. There's people queuing for days down there at the pass office.

The others exchange looks and mutters on how expertly CAN excuses himself.

Even Ma Bob got to have a permission to stay now, and she lived in Gerty Street since Adam. That right, Henry.

Henry Yeah, that's er, that's right Syl.

Bob That's it Mr Stein. I should know. Ma Bob's my…ma.

Surpressed giggles.

Syl This true? You've all got to have these stamps now?

Beat. All go to fetch out and hold up their passes – and SYL realises he has placed himself in an unfortunate position – and speaks to forestall it.

Alright, alright I'm not the polisie. Looks like I'm stuck with you all for the time being. I've had a few words with Jim Bailey. He agrees with me; the new edition is A-One stuff, the best yet. We've got coverage right across the board. We're good for another two editions at least. Thank you.

Can It's a pleasure Syl. They are a fine team, we pulled together, don't you say?

Syl Specially remarked on your contribution Henry. That was top drawer. Brave too. Ribs holding up OK?

Henry They're fine, Syl. Thanks.

Casey Those jail guards kick hard, hey Henry. For white people.

Syl So I told Jim we'd be having an indaba soon. Plan the further adventures of Mr Drum. We'll need some ideas. From everyone.

Casey You want us to get sorted for the indaba now, Syl?

Syl I reckon we should have a full house for this one. Todd and Zeke are back in next week. We'll do it then. Also, I want a word with Can here. In private.

Can Fine with me, Syl. Your office?

Syl Out here. Now. Rest of you, you can go. Reward for your work last month.

Bloke We didn't finish Dolly's mailbag yet, Syl…

Syl She'll keep. You too Henry. Maybe I'll see you round the Back o' the Moon when I finish up. Celebrate.

Can Mr Stein's right, we should celebrate this, boys. We owe Henry here.

Henry May-be, Syl. That would be very nice.

Come on boys. You heard Sylvester. There's enough wild stories been reported in here today. Let's go and make news at Fatty's. I might even buy you young bucks a drink.

Bloke   By the saints, how big was that bonus?

Casey   No questions, man, he's buying. Hey, Bob bring the camera – we might get some good snaps down there. 'Mr Drum's finest hour.'

Bloke   Yessir – 'The Drum boys introduce their readers to the illicit high life still jumping in Soph'town's lowlife districts.'

CASEY and BLOKE make to exit. Exit BOB to darkroom.

Syl   I mean it. Good work this month Henry.

Henry   No problem Syl. I'll see you later Canadoce.

Can   Go to it, Captain.

Casey   Bye, man.

Bloke   Rest in Peace, Canadoce...

All exit. Pregnant pause. CAN looks at the papers.

Can   We're not just some jazz-rag now, hey Syl?

Pause.

We can't talk in your office?

Syl   No. No, you see, that office – that's for senior editorial staff. That's me, and my Assistant Editor, Mr Can Themba. The smartest, best read, most talented newsman of his generation...

Can   Listen, Syl...

Syl No excuses. My assistant weighs in. He contributes. To do that, you have to be here, not leaving it to Henry and the others to come up with the goods.

Can Well, I'm here now Syl…

Syl Yes, now you are…

Can (*A feeble joke.*) 'Fore that I was coming…

Syl We pretty much got this one out without you. I'm not going to do that again. I made you Assistant Editor! That's an extra two pounds a week, and a desk in my office. Going AWOL for days on end then turning up with some cock-an-bull about being pulled over is not enough. These days, not nearly enough.

Can We're riding the wave aren't we?

Syl Yes, yes we are. Where the hell were you?

Can You know, when I told those guys at the Pass Office I work with the famous Mr Drum…

Syl They should sue you for bladdy perjury! The time you've spent here the last blerry month hardly… (bares thinking about)

O Christ, can we not get two minutes alone in here…?

CASEY, BLOKE, and HENRY all back-pedalling into the room.

Bloody hell boys, just stay out for five minutes, will you…!

They are followed in by two TSOTSIS in zoot suits. TSOTSI 1 brandishes a knife. They close the door behind them.

Tsotsi 1 Don't none of you skollies make no trouble or you fuckin' finished.

Tsotsi 2 Which one of you braves is it?

Tsotsi 1 I told you, man, it's him. Spot Mr Drum and claim your reward!

Tsotsi 2 Yeah? You him, hey. Mr Drum?

He is right in HENRY's face. He opens his flick knife.

I have my five pounds please?

TSOTSI 1 creases up.

Syl How d'you people get in here? Get out of my bladdy office!

Tsotsi 1 Woah, keep a lid on it Jewboy. This ain't wifey yo fucking with.

Syl (*Reacting.*) You what?!

Henry Woah, steady on there, brothers, it is me. Over here. You're right, fellas. I'm Mr Drum. Your business is with me. Right here.

HENRY walks away, taking off his hat, drawing attention to himself and away from SYL.

Can Hey. Have some respect man. It's me. I'm Mr Drum.

Casey You crazy sonofabitch – I'm Mr Drum.

Bloke The hell you are, half-jack – You boys want Mr Drum? ...He's off sick today...

Tsotsi 1 Shut up, you fuckers. There's one Mr Drum, right.

Tsotsi 2 This one?

Tsotsi 1 That's it. That's the face.

Tsotsi 2 You don't watch your mouth around town, asking questions, you gonna look like you had six train accidents. Verstaan?

Tsotsi 1 You get that Jewboy? Don't you even think about putting his stuff in your paper no more, man. Got that?

Syl Where's Bob? Hey Bob! Bob!

Enter BOB from the darkroom, pulling on a jacket. He notices the vital thing.

Bob I'm going Mr Stein, I don't want to miss…

Syl Camera, photo, quick.

BOB's reaction is almost instant. Prompted, he sizes up the scene and snaps the TSOTSIS.

Don't think we'll be using these pictures on the social page neither, gents. Now clear off, before I really lose my temper.

Tsotsi 1 Hang, you pushed me now Jewboy.

He puts his knife up to SYL's throat. TSOTSI 2 grabs the camera, and smashes it on the floor.

Bob Get off man! Don't…aw jeezus, man!

Syl You'd better let me go.

Can Yeah, you better had.

Tsotsi 2 You think your lanie skin gonna save you? From what I heard the cops give him a medal.

Tsotsi 1 We come for you all next time. Relocation? We pull this place down round your fucking ears. You verstaan that one?

Tsotsi 2 No man. I think Ol' Nxumalo here gonna forget that…

Tsotsi 1 Yeah?

Tsotsi 2 I think so.

He draws the blade across HENRY's hand. TSOTSI 1 is duly excited.

Tsotsi 1 Shit man! Now he remembers!! Six trains, man!!!

Tsotsi 2 We're leaving now.

He turns the knife on the others, before they can rush him. The TSOTSIS back out. HENRY feels the pain. Everyone rushes to his aid.

Casey Jesus!

Bob You OK Uncle Henry?

BLOKE is shocked at the sight of HENRY's blood.

Bloke Eina! They cut him man! They cut Henry!

Casey Hey, it ain't your blood, man, relax…

Henry I'm alright, man. It's nothing.

Syl (*Of TSOTSIS.*) Couple of meshuganners. You OK Henry?

Can Here, have a drink, man.

CAN passes a half-jack from his jacket to HENRY.

Henry Thanks bru that's kind.

HENRY takes a very long swig. BOB has retrieved the camera.

Bob I'll fix it up Mr Stein. I'm sorry…

Syl Don't worry about it, good work.

Can (*To HENRY.*) You OK there Bru?

Henry (*Finishes swig.*) I am now. Thanks.

Can Alright everybody. You can all go now. Casey, take Henry somewhere and get him a proper drink. The Ed and I are conversing in private…

Bloke You sure you OK Henry.

Casey No thanks to you, damn sicknote.

Syl He's fine, Bloke. Go on.

They file out. CAN lingers. When they're alone…

Can So…you were saying boss?

Beat. SYL's resolve collapses.

Syl Forget it. Have you slept at all lately?

Can Not much. I was going to organise a little musical
surprise for Henry, reward for all his labours last month.
Back o' the Moon probably.

Syl Go on then. Just be in early Monday.

Can Maybe we'll see you down there. Going to be quite a
night.

CAN exits.

Where you going, Hen?

HENRY comes back in.

Henry (*Calling over his shoulder.*) I'll be there.

Can (*Off, calling.*) Come on you guys, speed it up down
those stairs…

HENRY stops up short, seeing how shaken SYL is.

Henry You really OK, Sylvester?

Syl Do I look it? How's the hand?

Henry It's nothing, man. Couple of – what did you call
them? Meshuganners?

HENRY has picked up his hat.

Syl Is there something I should know about Henry? A new
story?

Beat.

Henry Aw it's nothing. Not yet anyway. I'll keep you posted though.

HENRY turns to exit.

Syl Be careful Henry. I don't think those skelms were joking.

Henry You know what the boys say. Live fast, die young, have a good-looking corpse.

    I'll see you later.

HENRY puts on his hat, and smiles, and exits.

Lights fade, with SYL running his hands over his face, shaken.

3

A spot picks out DOLLY as she sings, accompanied by TODD on piano.

A slow crooning song segues into jumping jazz.

Lights up to reveal we are in the Back o' the Moon shebeen. A couple of old and very battered sofas. On the first sit CASEY and BLOKE and HENRY.

On the second sofa, stretched out face-down and drunk beyond recall, is BOB.

As DOLLY sings, the guys clap along, whooping as CAN and LIZZIE dance the kwela.

All are smiling and happy – a good deal of drink has been taken, and HENRY is particularly glassy-eyed and mellow. More drinks are in hand or on a low table nearby.

The song ends and all applaud.

Lizzie Wow!

Henry Thank you Lizzie, that was very beautiful.

Lizzie My pleasure, Henry.

Henry As are you. Beautiful.

Lizzie Thank you again, Henry.

Can Say, you boys gonna make some space here, let the lady sit down?

Lizzie No, that's OK…

Casey It's no problem, Lizzie. Hold on Bobby, here we go.

Henry Gently gently… Lay him down gently, man.

CASEY drags BOB from the sofa to set him down behind it, while HENRY supervises.

Bloke You know, that was a song from the show, Lizzie. Todd's show. We all believe it will be a big success.

Lizzie It will be, I'm sure.

TODD arrives with a tray of drinks.

Todd We got more and more and more pin-ups!

Can You ever met Todd before…?

Lizzie No, I haven't…

Can He is a wonderful jazz composer – which is just as well, cause he's a terrible newsman…

Dolly But he's a barman you can trust.

Todd I always love to meet a beautiful lady. Especially one who is such a terribly bad judge of character…

Can You guys sharing courting lines?

Henry Come on and sit down next to me, Lizzie.

Everyone squashes onto the sofas – seats, arms, back – or sits on the floor nearby. What could be an awkward pause is headed off by LIZZIE – her salutation – correct in this company – is greeted well.

Lizzie Well. Gezundheit!

Henry She's got it!

All Gezundheit!

Todd Say…you didn't bring Mr Stein round with you guys?

Can Sylvester had quite enough action for one day…

Dolly That man is like a coiled spring waiting to go off. I may be just the girl to do it.

Henry If anyone could Dolly, it would be you.

Dolly He don't hurry, he's going to miss his chances. Me and Todd are going to be in New York, and you Drum boys are gonna be cold and lonely without us.

All laugh – slightly mocking this boast.

Can That's the plan, hey? You two getting away with the show?

Todd Well, maybe. It's getting tough being round here these days. The way things are.

This has touched a raw nerve. CASEY is oblivious.

Casey Y'know, we had a couple of Russians come in the Madhouse today. Real tsotsis. Meaner than the Americans' gang. Man, they knew what they wanted, those guys.

Lizzie What – gangsters?

Casey Coupla – what he call them?

Severally (*They all give different versions.*) Meshagunners / Moshiginnners / Mashugrinners…

More laughter.

Casey Stuck Henry with a knife – ow man! – on his hand there.

Dolly Why the tsotsis turning on you Henry?

Henry Yes, yes, just tsotsis. I keep telling these guys, it's nothing but a fleshwound. Besides, Can and these boys, they stood up for me; man's blessed to have friends like these.

Casey (*Admiring the TSOTSIS.*) They still got you knifed though hey Henry.

Lizzie What's that word meshagunners?

Can Mr Stein is of the Jewish disposition, my dear. He slips himself a bit of the Yiddish tongue now and then…

Todd Syl's the baas-man, Lizzie. He ain't seen Can inside a year…

Bloke What Todd means, my dear, is Sylvester's the editor of our magazine. And according to Can here, something of a Boy-scout.

Casey Well he ain't no damn sicknote, man.

Can Hey Todd, did you know Syl Stein was born in Cape Town?

Todd (*Straight man.*) No, I did not know that.

Can (*Pressing on with the gag.*) He was also born at night. Course, I don't know if it was last night…

All join in on the last line. Laughter.

Dolly He musta bin born last night, working with you guys…

Todd I second that, my dear. Mr Stein deserves our sympathy. Sylvester, and the all-conquering Drum.

All agree, raising their glasses in a toast.

All Sylvester/Drum.

Someone starts up a short song – a cappella – and all join in, clapping. It finishes and again all laugh and clap.

Bloke Ooo weee! (*Then unthinking.*) So tell us Lizzie, what did you do with your children tonight?

Henry Bloke, man!

Lizzie No it's OK… They're at school. Boarders. Michael – my husband – he's away on a field trip, in Cape Town.

Bloke The responsibilities of parenting are onerous, don't you find? I have a daughter myself, Lizzie…

Dolly So while the cat's at that, the mouse gets out. Right?

Can Steady my dear. You know, Mr Hutchinson is a very educated fellow. An artist. And a collector of art.

Bloke I have a broad taste in art too, Lizzie…

Dolly Whereas Can just has a taste for broads. Coloured girls, mostly. White girls are a special delicacy…

Beat.

Lizzie (*Defusing.*) I rather like the sound of that. Being chosen by a connoisseur is quite a compliment.

Can And believe me, she is the prize of my collection.

Casey (*Bitter laugh.*) They got you there Dolly.

Can I do hope not, man. Get one over on Dolly these days, I hear her new boyfriend's gonna come by and break my legs or something…

Henry Ooooh wee, steady there, Canadoce. I'm sure whatever Dolly's boyfriend is, he is a necessary professional connection. Not so, my dear?

Dolly He's just jealous Henry.

Can Why would I be jealous?

Dolly Because you're a man. Or what passes for one round here.

All Ooooh…

Can I don't hear Lizzie here moaning.

Lizzie That's right. (*Beat, then with a smile.*) Except in a good way…

Beat. They fall around, thigh-slapping pleasure in a good line.

Henry This girl is something! Yessir!

Todd They put something in the liquor here? I'm gonna play before you people start fighting each other…calm the savage breast as the poet said…

Dolly You do that Toddy.

TODD goes to the piano, and begins to play. HENRY stands – rather unsteadily – and makes an exaggeratedly formal request.

Henry May I have the pleasure of a dance, Dolly?

Dolly You want to dance with me? Here?

Henry Why not? You not as ugly as Casey.

Dolly OK. I hope you're ready for this…

CASEY stands.

Casey You say what about me, Henry??

39

Henry I didn't say nothing that ain't true. Sit down, half-jack.

Beat.

Casey You give that man a heart attack, you hear, Dolly?

Henry Gonna give us something to dance to, man?

Todd You got it.

DOLLY and HENRY dance. As soon as they begin, BLOKE leans or moves over.

Bloke I hope you won't mind what Dolly says, Lizzie. She shoots from the hip a little.

Casey Damn right she does. Man just look at those hips. White wages and the cover girl, how the hell does he do it man.

Lizzie I think she's great. Besides, it's nothing to what people call me these days. Especially in Westdene.

Bloke You live in Westdene?

Can That's it. Nice neighbourhood, don't you say?

Bloke You are ferociously brave to come to Soph'town Lizzie! And we are plain crazy to have you! Oooh look at Henry. I swear he is all of forty years. Now he's got the juice, he's like a young buck.

Can (*Adjusting his seat.*) That is the miracle of pin-ups, man. Fixes the mind on the good things of life. God dammit Casey. How the hang do you always get the best seat?

Casey Because you are not quick enough, man.

CASEY gets to his feet, with sudden (and sodden) determination.

Have the damn seat. If you know what you want, you go and get it, right?

Can (*Eyeing LIZZIE.*) S'right, man.

CASEY sets off toward the dancers. CAN realises what is going to happen.

O no leave them be, man… This is Henry's party…

CASEY ignores CAN, weaving his way toward the dancers and attempts to displace HENRY.

Casey I'm cutting in here man.

Henry No man, half-jack, I don't think so.

Casey The fuck I ain't!

Dolly Hang Casey, get your hand off me…!

Henry Now listen here, Kid…

Casey Half-Jack. Who the hell… (you calling half-jack!) You think you're the big-shot now, ja?

Dolly No, man…!

Can Hey, Casey!

CASEY lunges for HENRY, who dodges. CASEY regains his balance, and tries again. Again, HENRY dodges. Music has now stopped.

Henry Now you leave it there, Kid… C'mon Dolly…

HENRY starts to turn back to DOLLY. CASEY lunges a third time, HENRY sidesteps and this time unleashes a fearsome jab, straight out of the text book. CASEY is sent sprawling.

HENRY feels pain from his wounded – and now bruised – fist, heads for the door.

Bloke Hey, Captain, you breaking up the party already? Over a li'l turd like Casey?

Casey What's up with him, man? Nearly broke my fucking cheekbone!

HENRY kicks the door open and exits.

Can Hang Henry, wait up.

Casey Hey, it's me needs the help, man...he can hold his own...

CAN kicks the door open, and we are with him in the yard. Oil drums for mixing brews, an old bicycle, stray bits of corrugated steel. As CAN follows him out, HENRY feels his fist – the same one that was cut earlier.

Can You OK Henry?

Henry Shit...

Can Nice night for a ruck, hey.

HENRY gingerly inspects his wounded fist. CAN sits on a wall nearby.

Not your day, hey man.

Henry (*Ruefully.*) Man, it's always my day.

Pause.

Can They got something on you, Henry?

Henry Who – Casey?

Can Damn Tsotsis, man.

Henry You're as bad as Sylvester. I'll see you later.

HENRY aims to go back inside, but CAN detains him.

Can You got a light Henry?

Henry Sure, Catch.

Can You should get that nurse-wife of yours to look at that hand.

Henry You're all nurses. I told you, man, it's nothing.

Can Still getting it cold at home hey.

Beat. CAN now has HENRY's attention.

This bein' Mr Drum's dangerous, Bru. Bust ribs one day, knifewound at the office. Attacked when you go out. You sure you want to live with this aggravation all the time?

Henry If you are applying for the job, Mr Themba, I'll be happy to move over. Could be it's work to suit a younger man.

Can No no, I'm happy to leave all the hard news to you Henry. I just thought…

Henry What? What did you think?

Beat. This is more confrontational than CAN planned. He shakes his head.

Can Jeez, man. You've changed, you know that?

Henry Like the man said, a man changes the world, or the world changes him.

Can Yeah? Which is it with you these days?

Beat. HENRY takes out his pipe.

Henry So, how about my Bru, Canadoce? How does he find being Assistant Editor? Nice?

CAN cracks at this clear admonition.

Can O God, man. That Sylvester. Jeezus. Sometimes I think we should turn that office into a ring. Me and him. Baasman and the office boy, slug it out.

Henry You in the ring? I'd pay money to see that. You know, Sylvester's just trying to keep the paper going, do a mean job with this mean lot of people.

43

Can Mean like you, hey. That why you betting on Gerty Street to go the distance? You gone soft man. When I started at Drum, life with Henry was one long day at the dog track, free drinks and pretty smiles. Not one care in the damn world. Now here you are being a 'Journalist'. Something went badly wrong with you, man.

Henry And here's you, Shakespeare of the Shebeens, being…what, exactly? Absent mostly.

They exchange smiles. They are now in a more comfortable space.

Can You know what ol' Sartre would say about all this Mr Drum nonsense?

Henry No, Bru, I don't. But I guess you're going to tell me…

Can That's what you might call, 'denying the self'. You are sublimating your sovereign will to an external ideology – ideology of opposition in this case. Idea that a man must fight injustice in order to be a man. Whereas, the liberated man, the existential man…

Henry I'm guessing this is you, hey Canadoce.

Can – the existential man makes his own choices, reinventing himself as he goes, regardless of the world he is in. The free man, the true bohemian, lives according only to his will.

Henry This is the same Sartre fought with the French resistance, hey?

HENRY strikes a match, re-lighting his pipe. Beat.

We are all living undercover in this place, man. Every last native. Even that damn fool Casey.

Can Not Can Themba. I've blown my cover wide open. I am living the life of a free man. My Lizzie is proof of that, don't you say?

44

Henry She is quite a girl. I'm talking about a cover that crushes.

You ever heard of Black Velvet?

Can (*Making light.*) That's what, a new cocktail.

Henry No no, it's a kind of a game. The cops pick up a goodtime girl and her white customer. The white guy, they let him go with a warning – about all the laws he is breaking and the disease he is catching, going with a dirty native girl. The girl herself, they let her off completely. Yessir. All she has to do, to regain a touch of this freedom you talk about, is give those white cops a free ride in the back of the kwela kwela. One cop, then the other, then the other one…then the boy from the garage with a piece of hose pipe, and so forth. By the time they've done taking this native woman off the street, there's not much velvet left.

Beat.

Can Jeez Henry, there you go again, man. Are you the conscience of the nation now?

Henry If we don't find a way to live like men, we gonna end up like beetlejuice, nothing but dribble down a whiteman's chin. There won't be a Sof'town then. There won't be nothing at all.

Beat.

Can Lucky old Narcissus, hey Henry.

Henry Ja, damn that lucky bastard.

Beat. HENRY cracks into a smile – this is something they've said before. They are back to being buddies.

Can You shared these revolutionary feelings with Sylvester lately?

Henry Hang, no. I wouldn't want to embarrass the man.

45

They smile.

And by the way, you brought Dolly here tonight? I know what that is, and I do appreciate the gesture, but…

Over CAN's shoulder the door opens, and LIZZIE enters. HENRY is all smiles.

Lizzie Am I safe to come out here…?

Henry Hey now, I'm guessing this is that Lizzie come to see where her man got to.

Lizzie That's me.

Henry You know you kids should be careful. The cops see you out in the yard enjoying mixed-race conversation, I don't care to think but they going to lock you up in some nasty gaol cell, Miss Hutchinson. That can be unpleasant.

Lizzie It's alright. I know what that's like…not just from reading Mr Drum either.

Henry What's that?

Can You didn't hear? Lizzie done almost as much chooky as you Henry.

Henry You did?

Lizzie Don't listen, it was just a weekend.

Henry Just a weekend? For talking to man like Can Themba? That is a crime, young lady!

Lizzie I was at a party that got raided, that's all. It's my own fault. I insist on mixing with the wrong people. (*Scarf back on.*)

Now I have to wear my protective veil, pass for a Coloured…

Henry Well, I see you are an old hand in Sof'town already. You take care all the same, Lizzie. The police catch Can out after the curfew again, he's in big trouble. I'll see you soon. Good to have you around Lizzie.

Lizzie You too Henry. We'll be in soon.

HENRY starts to exit, CAN calling after.

Can Hey Henry, Dolly moving through the gears OK tonight?

Henry O our Dolly, she is a regular well-upholstered chevvy!

HENRY exits. CAN and LIZZIE exchange smiles, then CAN looks down.

Lizzie Everything OK?

Can Oh, he will be; few more pin-ups. Little more Dolly.

(*Snapping out.*) Hang. He should be OK. I know I am.

CAN kisses her.

C'mon it's cold out here. Let's show Dolly how you dance the kwela.

Lizzie Ah no, not again, Dolly's much too good –

The door has burst open. CASEY, BLOKE, TODD, come racing out and leaping over fences, all whooping and yelling 'Go!' 'Go man!!', HENRY is following.

Can C'mon...hey! careful man! Wass the hurry?

Henry Police! Go!

Lizzie What?

The sound of police whistles fills the air. CAN laughs.

Can Hang, you put the hex on us Lizzie.

LIZZIE makes to run toward the back gate, but CAN grabs her hand.

No, it's covered that way – kitchen go! Go!

Blackout. Spot on dustbin lid, spinning to a halt; all that remains…

4

The Office. Monday, 31 December, morning.

CAN is sitting at a desk, concentrating intensely on a magnificent house of cards he is building on his desk. He is adding the final two cards…

CASEY standing/sitting nearby, similarly concentrating.

SYL enters arriving for work, carrying his briefcase. He sees CAN, then looks around him, amazed that no one else is around.

Syl Morning boys.

Casey Sssshh.

Can Hey, manners Casey. Hoozit, Syl.

Syl Hoozit. You two in before Henry?

Casey Captain had to go to Marshall Square this morning. Get young Bob out of chooky.

Syl Bob? Oh Jesus!

Casey He got lost behind the sofa.

Can Poor Bob had the misfortune to be at the Back o' the Moon just when Fatty got herself raided, Friday night.

Syl O, jeez. Anyone else get nabbed?

Casey Just Bobby.

Can Hence my model of that grand old club.

SYL steps forward.

Syl That's quite a work of art, Themba. Glad to see arriving at work early wasn't entirely wasted.

Can Ah!

Casey Careful boss – floor's shaky there.

Syl (*Sorry.*) Right.

Can The Good ol' Back o' the Moon. Accurate in every detail.

Syl I see. That's a tin roof, is it?

Can Exits one two three four and five. That one here's my favourite. That's the kitchen window. Through which my love and I fled for a weekend of existential and if I may say it, romantic abandon.

Casey Whereas I was forced to exit over the fence. Through the garbage.

Syl That where you got the shiner? From the polisie?

Casey Not exactly…

Can That was a misunderstanding with one of the boys.

Syl It takes a steady nerve, to live your kind of life, hey.

Can It does. Course, there's not another life being offered just now. If the Resettlement program progresses, Fatty's will look quite different to this model.

Syl Right.

Can Once those bulldozers reach Gibson Street there'll just be a clean, white, empty space.

CAN lifts up the pyramid clean off the desk – all glued in one piece. SYL realises he's been had.

49

Syl O lumme. You rotters…

He lets them have their laugh.

Can Welcome to the madhouse, Syl.

Syl (*Hopeful.*) You're not joking about Bobby though are you?

Can Fraid not.

Casey (*Reassuring.*) They'll be here, Syl.

Syl Ja well. I hope so. We need to get our heads together. Sore or not.

SYL goes into his office, calling to BLOKE as he goes.

Morning Bloke.

BLOKE enters.

Bloke Bon jour Monsieur Stein. Morning, mes amis.

Can Hey Modisane.

Bloke Hey Motsisi. Here's today's paper; you can check on the latest odds.

He throws it on CASEY's desk where it lies.

Casey Ta, Bloke. (*To CAN, sotto.*) What about it?

Can (*Sotto.*) Nah. Too late. Hey Bloke. Anyone else coming up?

Bloke Zeke and Todd right behind.

Casey Yes man…!

Bloke Wass going on?

Can Ssssh!

Todd (*Off.*) No man, I swear, this black guy used to be a coloured girl…

Zeke Sure, sure…

Enter ZEKE, carrying a briefcase, followed by TODD.

Can Hoozit Zeke. Good to see you.

Zeke Good to see you, yes. Morning dear chap.

Casey Having a holiday last week?

Zeke No no. No Casey, there was some course-work I needed to catch up with. What's going on over there?

Casey O, It's just a thing Can made this morning. Want to see it?

Can Careful Casey – floor's a wee bit shaky just there.

Casey Ja, sorry man. Don't breathe too heavy, ja? Things have reached a delicate stage.

TODD, ZEKE and BLOKE join the huddle around CAN's masterpiece.

Todd Hey thass not bad man. You don't get the shakes in the morning?

Can I do, till I get a drink. Model of Fatty's, over in Gibson Street.

Casey (*Explaining to ZEKE.*) We got raided there Friday. Bobby's in chooky.

Zeke You don't say? Goodness Casey. Now this work of art of yours, it certainly seems a well-turned design you know.

Can Exits one two three and four.

Todd Pity I didn't find no damn exit. Cost me a whole load of tickets, keep me out of clink.

Casey What do you say Old E'Zekie, life-like too, hey.

Zeke Mmm, I'm not so sure – not being a shebeen kind of man. But I'd say it was better built than the real thing...

Having peered closely, ZEKE has now picked the whole thing up.

Can O jeez, Mphahlele...a person can't have any fun with you around.

Bloke He got you there, man!

BLOKE's head slowly droops as he starts to doze off.

Zeke That's my mission – global misery and sadness. You would have to rise very early to fool Ezekiel Mphalele my friends. Where's Henry.

Casey Fetchin' Bobby out of Marshall Square. Flashing his chief reporter's pass and tugging his hair out.

Zeke You and Henry are leading that boy astray you know that Can Themba. Just like you ruined Casey here.

Can What do you say Toddy-boy. Are we a bad influence on Bobby?

Todd F sharp. Modulating. What?

Zeke Ja, very well, go ahead, drink yourselves stupid. I don't suppose anyone'll miss a couple more educated males of potential.

Casey Bloke's kind of quiet today too. You OK Modisane?

Bloke (*Wakes up.*) Juss – resting my eyes, boys. I have a hang of a babbelas! Turned into quite a weekend, I'm happy to say. Planning some rather Debonaire entertainment, for the next few days...

SYL returns. BLOKE sits up sharply, feet off desk.

Syl Alright. Still no Henry hey. You boys got a rota going?

Casey That's it. Guess we'll just have to play with the hand of cards life deals us.

Syl Great. Morning Zeke. How was college.

Zeke O it's going fine, Syl. It's stimulating.

Syl Unlike here, you mean.

Zeke No no not at all. And you, Sylvester?

Syl Fine, thanks. Usual pressures.

Zeke Hmm. You got away for the weekend though I hope?

Syl Er, yes. Thanks.

Zeke The Cape this time?

Syl No, er, Durban actually.

Zeke That is nice

Beat. SYL's discomfort is tangible.

Syl (*Ploughing on.*) Alright so let's get started. Todd, Bloke.

Bloke I'm here Syl, always listening.

Todd Here Mr Stein.

Syl Can's contribution. Promptly submitted.

'I joyed as I passed into Hoek Street, seeing the white girls coming up King George Street, the sunlight striking through their dresses, articulating the silhouettes beneath to show me leg and form; things blackmen are supposed to know nothing of, and which the law asininely decrees may not even be imagined' …and later… 'That night I went to bed (*He falters slightly.*) with…Lottie…Lottie with that tinkling English voice, we went to bed together, she and me…together, chocolate on cream.'

Bloke Ooo whee, you hit it hot there Canadoce!

Casey You two sure in the open now, man!

Syl Last month an article on the Russians gang from Henry, this time sex across the colour bar.

Can It is a heady mix, don't you say.

Syl And not based on the life of anyone we know…? (*Referring to the story.*) Taking this English girl to a shebeen, and after the revenge of a Zulu girlfriend.

Can Attempted revenge. Happily the cops ignored Bibi's complaints. I'm now officially a free man.

Syl Autobiographical.

Can My tale is based on people with whom I am acquainted, somewhat. Like all the best fiction.

Todd Sounds like opera to me…

Bloke Yeah, man, her real name's Brunhilde.

Casey I tell you, Syl, this Lizzie slips through a window like a hand past silk.

Syl An English woman, called Lizzie, running around Sophiatown…

Zeke It's as you said Syl, last time the Russians gang, this time Inglese. Sex, violence, why not promote these lanie pleasure seekers?

Syl This wouldn't be Lizzie Hutchinson would it?

Can That is the lady's name. Says she knows you somewhat, as a matter of fact. In the social sense.

Syl No, not really. But I do know her husband.

Beat.

Can Yes I did meet the man one time. Artist. A pleasant man.

Casey You met the man?

Bloke Heh heh, why not, they got soooo much in common now.

Syl Alright. Nice writing Can, but I can't publish it.

Can Aw come on Syl...

Syl Like I said it's nice writing. Provocative too. But it's just not possible. Not now. Sorry.

Casey Aw come on Syl you said circulation was up last week. Why, man? Cause we give the readers excitement!

Zeke Cause you give them a diet of salacious low-living.

Syl If we publish anything promoting illegal acts, in Sophiatown, we'll be closed. Quite apart from the innocent people endangered...

Can Hang man, Lizzie knows the score, my life is research. Besides, we're always in trouble. That's the game. This is Drum Magazine, man, not the damn Housewife.

Beat. SYL has to make a decision.

Zeke I'm with you Syl, if the Nats want to close Drum down, why not get closed for something worthwhile, not this trashiness.

Beat.

Syl What else have we got...

Zeke O really, you know boys, I don't know why I ever come back here...

Casey There's something we agree on...

ZEKE has stood as if to leave. Enter HENRY.

Syl Ah Henry. Siddown, we made a start. Bob OK?

Henry Sure, Syl. They let him out.

Enter BOB, dishevelled, bruised.

Casey Been in chooky hey Bob? Be a legend like your
Uncle soon.

Can You OK Bob?

Bob Sure.

*HENRY sits down heavily, hat in hand, shell-shocked. SYL
continues, oblivious.*

Syl Alright, so, we'll come back to Can's stuff. What else…

Can Wo woah…what's going on? You boy's alright?
Henry? What is it man?

Beat.

Henry Ma-Bob woke up just before light. Where a
sledgehammer took her door in. House she lived in
twenty-three years. (*Beat.*) Gerty Street, Miller, some in
Gold Street. They're gone.

*Pause. CASEY very deliberately takes out a five pound
note.*

Casey You say Gerty Street? That is a result for me, man.

He picks up his jacket, then sees the faces of the others.

Well, do we get the damn story or not?

*HENRY gets up and goes to his desk, pulls open his drawer
and pulls out a new pad, a pen, slaps them on the desk.
Closes the drawer, picks up pad and pen. He gestures toward
CASEY.*

Henry He stays. Someone do something with him.

Exit HENRY. Blackout.

5

A typewriter chatters. Lights up on the office, two hours later. Door open.

CASEY is bound and gagged, tied to a chair.

CAN slouched in his seat, absently picking apart the house of cards, periodically skimming the cards across the room, to hit CASEY.

HENRY is typing with calm focus, hat still on, pipe clenched between his teeth.

TODD, ZEKE, seated or standing around HENRY as he types.

All (bar CASEY) are wearing coats – it's been raining outside.

Enter BLOKE and BOB. BLOKE talks to anyone who will listen.

Bloke Man! Ok, I was ready for bulldozers, a coach load of cops...but I saw this one house, true's God, they had a – what's that thing Bobby? – a, a, a tank barrel, through the damn roof! They got the whole damn army down here!

No one is listening. Offstage, in SYL's office a phone is slammed down.

Syl (*Off.*) Fucking blarry piesang!

Everyone pauses.

Bloke Who the hang's he talking to?

SYL enters from his office. Beat.

Syl Jim Bailey. Who else?

Beat.

What's up. Never heard me swear before?

Carry on.

HENRY continues his typing. BLOKE moves to see it.

Bloke Ach no, Syl, you simply gotter stop this. They'll call this incitement to opposing! We report on this, we'll be history, man.

Todd If we don't tell the story of our times we'll be history anyway, Modisane.

Zeke …You're absolutely damn right.

(*To HENRY.*) You missed a stop there.

Syl You manage to get me the business with the tank, Bob?

Bob Ja well, sort of. I only had the Leica, but it should be OK.

Syl So we've got pictures, we've got copy. Alright. So. We cover it as a news item.

Beat – typing stops.

Henry What?

Zeke What – and no opinion piece?!

Todd Yes, if not from us, at least from Chief Luthuli or someone!

Syl It'll be clear enough what Drum's position is. Henry's account will make it clear. Clear as it can be. Right Henry?

HENRY regards SYL levelly, taps out his pipe, passes it over for a refill. TODD obliges – tobacco, lighting, puffing.

Henry Pretty well. Clear to who, is the question.

Bloke Clear position hey, Syl, Ja man… With a bullseye round my neck. I need this job man. If I lose this job, I lose my stamp. I got events planned!

Todd (*Calmly, puffing the pipe into action.*) If your Landlord gets 'resettlemented' out of his house, you lose the damn stamp anyway, man.

Bloke But what could I do about that – I couldn't stop no tank. Or no Landlord. I need my position here!

Zeke What you need Bloke is a blessed backbone. Just like Casey here needs a little sensitivity.

Casey Nnng.

The others glance at CASEY, and if they react at all, it's with a callous, dismissive smile.

Syl It'll be clear to the readers, home and abroad what's happening. That's enough.

Zeke (*To BLOKE.*) You know people are losing their homes every day, man. Last place any African can own a piece of this damn country.

Bloke Man, you think I don't know that? My home will be next, it's not going to be me living out in ruddy Orlando!

Zeke Good enough for others – not good enough for a play-white, hey?

Bloke Who the hell're you calling play-white?!

They have squared up.

Syl Sit down, Bloke. Sit down both of you. Sit!

Beat. CAN sends another card winging towards CASEY – hopefully hitting him.

Henry Sit down, Bloke.

Beat. BLOKE crumples into a chair. ZEKE follows suit. But BLOKE can't stay sitting, and immediately jumps up.

Bloke I just need this bloody job!

Syl We all need the bloody job or we wouldn't bloody be here!! Now sit down!

Beat. BLOKE is completely crumpled by this outburst. The shock is general; a line has been crossed, as SYL is acutely aware.

(*Trying to continue.*) Look, they could have gagged Drum any time in the past year. They never do it. Why not?

Zeke Because we don't publish anything that really shakes the damn government. Sex, violence and sports reports, they're happy with that stuff.

Syl Maybe it's because we have intelligent readers, outside South Africa.

Groans, including CASEY – this is an old chestnut.

Syl Pretoria cares what London thinks, that's true. Isn't it?

Zeke (*Conceding the point.*) Certainly, Syl. So what.

Syl So. We deal with this as a news story, hard news, and we find a different way to underline what's going on. One the baboons from the Department of Security won't pick up on. Most important of all, we wrap it in a hell of an issue.

Bloke …Yeah, man, probably our last.

Syl It could be our last. But as Jim Bailey has made clear – he wants us to keep on selling lots of copies. That's what a newspaper's for. And that's true too, after all.

Zeke We have a hell of a story now, Syl. Let's go with it.

Syl If we incite anyone to oppose the government, we're in trouble. Criminal Law Amendment Act. As Jim Bailey says –

Zeke 'News is sacred, comment is free.' Man, he's the owner. Drum's just property to him.

Syl We can inform, we can't campaign. I say, we need a whole issue, not just a story. Worldwide attention, remember.

Order regained, if a sullen one, SYL starts the indaba.

Now then. Henry? Those Tsotsis we entertained the other day… Is this abortion story still hot?

Henry For sure, man.

HENRY rips his copy from the typrewriter, passes it to SYL.

I'll get to it.

Bloke The what story?

Syl D'you want to tell us about it?

Beat. HENRY sees no alternative but to play his part. He tells the others.

Henry There's a nurse my missus works with. Florence heard her at the hospital talking about some lowlife surgeon she met. Could be this doctor is the Mr Big in the abortion game. So I nosed around a little. Means we can do a white crime piece for a change.

Syl White doctor makes money from native misery. That's good. The Department of Security won't like it, but if it's a crime story we're on safe ground. Be careful, make sure the sources check out. Who else? Toddie: Music scene.

Todd Fixed up, Syl. My story's I.D.B. In the bag. Exclusive one-to-one with… Ladies and gentleman, the Queen of Kwela, the singing canary (*Showing picture.*) Miss Dolly Rathebe.

Can Boosting the show, hey Toddie?

Todd Not at all, man.

Syl What a girl. Dolly suit you OK Zeke?

ZEKE is forced to smile.

Excellent, jazz 'em up with prose. Go easy on the James Joyce bits though. Any new pix of Dolly?

Bob Today, Syl. Got the camera fixed up now, sort of.

Can Advance copies, five bob apiece, hey Bob.

Bob Well, sort of.

Syl Wunderbar. Alright. Political interest, Zeke?

Zeke Political Disinterest. I did have an interview with Professor Mabuso arranged; ANC opposition to the clearing of Sophiatown. I'm going to change that now. 'Why is the ANC like an old comb?'

Syl Good. Nice tone. Play it down the middle, let's not lose contact. The ANC are allies. Casey – Soccer.

Zeke Soccer??!

Syl Like I said, the whole darn issue. Casey?

CASEY nods.

Boxing – next big fight?

Casey (*Nodding again.*) Nnng.

Syl Social anyone? Bloke?'

Bloke IDB and all wrapped up. If I can take you into my confidence Syl, going to be rather splendid.

Syl Good. I like your fancy new byline by the way. Bloke Debonaire Modisane. If we can find a way to position it, we might just use Can's love story too – human interest. We need something on the off-beat side... Any ideas? Casey?

CASEY shakes his head.

Bob I saw this woman over Alexandra way, passing a snake through her face – in one nostril out the other.

Syl Sounds twanky enough. Photo by the end of the week. Alright, So. Back to the main feature. Anyone?

Bloke Don't you wanna lead with the abortion thing?

Syl I'm after something as strong as Henry's jail piece. Brave, and clever. Convince me that Resettlement, these bulldozers, the whole idea of Separate Development is not a better life for Africans. Undermine the tanks. Ridicule the government line. Come on! Do it!

Pause, all facing the challenge with varying degrees of enthusiasm.

Zeke How about historical.

Syl What – a context piece?

Zeke A context piece, ja. Jo'burg grows and grows through the sweat of the kaffir – so when Sof'town is founded in 1897…

Groaning; this is not exactly entertainment. ZEKE merely shouts louder.

…Africans are allowed to buy their own land cause they are five miles from the whites…NOW the Nats want everyone the hell out to Meadowlands, twelve miles away, that splits them up. Divide and rule!

Syl Alright, alright; good angle, wrong flavour. Why don't they close us down? Come on why are we still here at all, boys?

Bloke Man we been through this Syl…

Syl Can? Are we going have the benefit of your attention?

Can (*Rote.*) Drum Magazine is cheeky. We stick out the tongue, more than the neck.

Todd That's it.

Syl Good. Yup. So, to expose farmworkers' conditions, Henry here goes to the Boer farmer's back door…

Henry …and asks for work.

Todd 'I need work my-basie.'

Zeke …and by his beatings, and his other wicked deeds, the boer betrays himself.

Syl Right. When we get to prison conditions –

Todd Mr Drum here deliberately gets himself arrested.

Syl So. What does Mr Drum do this time. Henry?

Henry Thinking cap, Syl.

Syl Anyone else? Come on Zeke, let's give the lie to the helping hand. Are the goons in the Native Affairs Department really out to help us? Anyone?

Todd How about this, Syl. I'm thinking, counterpoint. Mr Drum takes some African kids for a dip on one of those old whites-only beaches. Durban or somewhere. Kids get kicked off the beach, and we get a jackpot. Hotspot or Blackspot, they just want our black ass gone!

Syl Illegal. Jim feels we should keep on the right side of the law just now. Avoid unnecessary confrontation.

Zeke Unnecessary?!

Syl He's in a difficult position…

Zeke They're using tanks and bulldozers and we have to stay legal!

Syl If we don't we may lose the magazine completely! Then we'll all be in chooky, or under house arrest.

CASEY emits muffled protest.

Casey Nnnng. Mnng. Pfgnn. Gmnph.

Bloke It's like Casey says, man, we are goin' to lose the magazine whatever we do…

Syl Come on, let's keep going. Bob? Any thoughts?

Bob Well, er OK Syl. They took all the houses in Gerty Street so far cept this one house that's an old Shebeen. Called The Sanctuary. I think the police are on the take, man. If we can prove it…

Zeke Prove it?

Todd What is there to prove, man?

Syl Not really a Mr Drum case, Bob. Nice idea though. What else…

Can Woah woah not so fast, boys. Maybe Bob here just turned prophet. Sanctuary. How about this. Mr Drum turns in penitence, an' throws himself upon the mercy of the church.

Bob (*Confused.*) It's a shebeen. The Sanctuary, you've been there, man…

Can No no no, listen. I was walking past this Church in Westdene.

Bloke Man you're the damn play-white! Westdene?!

Can (*Continuing.*) I was walking past this Afrikaner House of God and I seen this sign, a sign, brothers, big sign on the front. 'The Lord Gives Sanctuary To The Sinner.' It's not the beach we should be looking at Toddy-boy. How about we go for the Achilles heel of the whole damn thing. If I may mix my mythologies, the forehead of the entire damn Goliath. The church.

Todd Mess with the church? All those teetotallers? Say, I think Henry rather go shark-wrestling at the beach.

Can White churches don't oppose the Resettlement, why not? Is that Christian? Bloke?

Bloke I dunno man. They're too busy praying.

Zeke No, man! They call it slum clearance! So it sounds like missionary work!

Can That's it. But the truth is, they are for Resettlement. Get those damn kaffirs off our stoep. But doesn't the Word say, the church is here for every person? Every last sinner. Even a sinner as far beyond redemption as Mr Drum, what with his showgirls and his wide-boy associates and all his damn kaffir cheek. Right? Let's call it.

Bob How we going to do that?

CAN unties CASEY's gag.

Can Like the man said, he gets religion.

Bloke Like who said, man?

Can Regardless of age, income, sex, and colour, the church has to let you in, and to a warm embrace. Brothers in Christ.

Bloke Yeah man, in theory.

Can There you are, boys. It's neat.

CAN sits down, feet on desk, pleased with a problem solved.

Syl Is it? Is it that neat?

Bob I don't geddit. I go to church every Sunday with my ma. Where's the story?

Casey (*Spitting fluff from his mouth.*) You don't listen man – he's talking about a lanie church. One of you swells untie the rest now? Please?

Henry Native in Father Huddleston's church – no story. Native in a white church in Westdene…

Bloke – Yessir, we got all kinds of commotion!

Bob Well, you just gonna get throwed out, Bloke.

Casey Damn right you stupid b. It's not illegal, but you are still going to be bounced on your backside, cause they are the same people wiping us out of Sof'town. Please, man? Free the damn slave will you?

CAN obliges.

Bob Not me man. I'm not going in to no white church.

Syl Well. It's Cheeky.

Bloke Big story, man! And no rough stuff! You know, I think I would make an excellent Mr Drum, Syl. Conversing on a equal plane with these good, God-fearing people…

Zeke Equal plane? Man, those Afrikaaners'll be on fire, not to let Mr Drum get their nice clean church all dirty with his backside. We'll probably start a war right there on the boer's church steps!

Bloke Hey, no war-talk man, I'm a man of peace…

Todd We not talking war are we Syl?

Syl Boys, don't get carried away, alright. A simple act of defiance. Not even illegal. How do you like it, Casey?

Casey (*Wryly, feeling his sore wrists.*) Like they say, it's neat. Drum flavour. If anyone wants my opinion…

Syl Will it get a reaction?

Zeke All that righteous zeal. We're bound to, man. It's certain.

Todd He's right man, it's good.

67

Syl How about Henry?

Henry Church on one page, tanks on the other. 'Kaffirs not wanted at this address.'

Bob Sweet little pictures, man.

Henry Story of our times, I say.

Syl Could be useful to have a lanie editor for once. I get inside the Church with the Leica, snap a few candid close-ups.

Casey Mr Stein goes to church. At last, the Jewish gets converted.

Syl Bob'll be outside with the main camera, to watch the exit. We cable the pix to the world's press, and Can writes it up for us. His idea. Alright with you Can?

Can Shakespeare of the Shebeens. At your service.

Syl Good.

Bloke So what – do I get to be Mr Drum this time? No joking, man, I could do it. This is exactly my kind of mission.

Todd It was Can's idea, man.

Can I'm happy to forgo my chance for fame on this occasion – for Henry's sake.

Bloke Aw what?!

Syl He's right. It's no war, but the Boers could dish out quite a beating. Not really your scene, hey Bloke.

Casey Yeah man. We can't afford no (*Impersonates BLOKE.*) 'Mr Drum's off sick today…'

Syl You happy to keep the part for us Henry? Be Mr Drum again?

Henry Live fast, die young, have a good-looking corpse. I'll do it.

Bloke O man, he gets another damn bonus!

Todd That's it! Gents, I can just see the faces of those old respectables when Henry sits on their pew, hey?

Casey Yeah, and the missuses: (*Afrikaner accent.*) 'O hemel, dames en here, cleanin' rota's gone all to crap.'

Syl Excellent. We'll have a run-through of the practicals next week. Choose a date, pick out a church. Any questions?

Bloke Yeah – when do we get white wages…?

Syl Alright. Indaba closed. Thanks boys. And thanks Can. We've all got work to do. Let's get to it.

SYL exits to his office. All start to picking up coats, briefcases etc. HENRY's copy has arrived into CAN's hands. HENRY goes over to CAN's desk.

Henry Nice work, Can.

Can You too man. Mr Drum rides again.

Henry (*Private.*) Listen, are you going to be around tonight?

Can Not tonight man, I have a date with paradise.

Henry Again? (*Smiling wryly.*) So, how about a warm-up drink, this afternoon sometime?

Can Mmm, I'll be around. What's up? Cold feet already? Hey, I'm sorry about Ma-Bob. She be OK?

Henry No no, it's er it's a different matter Canadoce. Something I'm…wrestling with, just now.

Can House of Truth's always open for you Henry.

Henry Thank you Bru. I'll repay that favour some time.

SYL emerges, with papers in hand and is dismayed to see everyone leave.

Syl Where are you all going? It's not even two o'bally clock yet!

Henry O it's er New Year's Eve, Syl. Mr Bailey always lets us off early the day before New Year's.

Can Ja, ja, that's right. Specially now we've got our little plan together, hey Syl.

Henry All this talk of church does makes a man dry, don't you find?

Lights down.

6

LIZZIE's flat. 1 January 1957. Very early in the morning, the first light of dawn pouring through the open window. CAN and LIZZIE, semi-clothed, are smooching slowly to a record – township jazz, of course. They are exhausted. The record finishes and LIZZIE looks up.

Lizzie Hey hey. Wake up. Happy tomorrow.

Happy New Year.

They kiss, then groan and collapse onto the bed.

Neighbours will go mad.

Can Lady, this is Westdene. They already mad.

They laugh, kissing, pecking, snapping, playful kisses. He lies back, her finger tracing on his chest.

Lizzie One little black boy, hidden in the woodpile…

Did you ever play that game, 'Guess the picture'?

She draws.

Can Are you practising anatomy my dear, or drawing a heart for some other, foolish reason.

She jabs him with the finger – a gentle shot.

Lizzie Pig. I want to reach yours, that's all. I know it's in there somewhere.

Can You should've come to my house like I said. Consummate our affections in the House of Truth.

They smile. Suddenly decisive, LIZZIE sits up, putting her hair back up again, later lighting a cigarette. Throughout she maintains the same, bright tone.

Lizzie You should come to London this year. You'd love it.

Can What?

Lizzie I'm just saying. You're always going on about what's his name: Victor Hugo, Dickens – people in England don't read Dickens you know. Very passé. Anyway I've decided, Sophiatown is London. In the Jacobean period. With pavements.

Can Pavements…of all the twisted desires of my degenerate soul I have never ever lusted for a pavement. Though I confess, I have been made to kiss a few.

Lizzie We have cops too, even tsotsis – we call them Teddy Boys.

Can Teddy Boys?

Lizzie Knife fights, jazz, more squalor than you can believe, London is perfect for every kind of artist. You'd never want for being miserable in London, ever.

Can And the African artist?

Lizzie Black, brown, yellow – nobody cares. Nobody gives a damn in London what you are.

Can (*Drily.*) Ja, I heard that.

Beat.

Lizzie (*More serious.*) Can, you can't take responsibility for evrything this country does.

Can I thought you were in love with this country, Lizzie.

Beat.

Lizzie In Soho, a man can walk the streets with anyone he chooses. Another man, if he wants.

Can That is a tantalising thought, Mrs Hutchinson…

Lizzie Even with me. People would hardly notice. You'd love it.

Can And what work would this invisible homosexual African be doing in London? In this Sophiatown-with-pavements?

Lizzie All sorts. There's the University. I've got contacts – well Michael has – a visiting Lectureship – how about that? You'd have students hanging on your every word. You'd be insufferable.

Can They do get female students there, right?

Lizzie Swine! You can sell clothes pegs.

Can And clothes to wear? How can I survive away from my outfitters, girl?

Lizzie The best. Savile Row, if you like. They'll have you double breasted and pinstriped before you can draw breath. Opera, jazz clubs, there's everything. Theatre if you want it.

Can And if I don't?

Lizzie Cinema. Think of that, Can. Films with corrupting scenes left in. You'd love London.

Can Shebeens?

Lizzie Thousands. Bars anyway. Though the Queen's
Head doesn't really compare with Seventh Heaven or
Cabin in the Sky.

Beat.

Can And Mister Hutchinson? Is he going to be there? How
will he feel with me in Soho, his wife on my one arm,
my male lover on the other? Looking him in the eye as
an equal?

Lizzie He's an artist, he's a liberal.

Can He's a man though, ja?

Beat.

Lizzie Ja. You're right. Impossible. We'll just have to stay
here and go down with the ship.

They kiss again, still playful. Beat.

It's just so horrible downtown now. Soldiers… Rubble…

Can That's the way it is, girl. She's going down one street
at a time, that's one thing.

Lizzie That's worse. The creeping death. The creeping
bloody paralysis. They cut the houses down so they can
spy on people better. All those stupid looks I get. The
only place I feel safe is here, with you.

She lays her head on him. Pause.

Can I ever tell you I went to the coast this time? Casey and
me. There were these fishermen along the beach from
us. They caught a great octopus – great, massive thing.
They chopped off a tentacle, sold it to us, so we could
eat that night. Next day, we saw the octopus was still
alive, down there in the bucket. So we bought another
tentacle. Next day, the same thing. By the fourth day,
when we looked into the bucket, we could see the first
tentacle was growing again.

73

Lizzie That's disgusting.

Can No, no, it's a marvellous thing. If a octopus is healthy, it grows the leg right back again. Me and Casey, we said to each other, Hang, if we could afford that whole beast, and we could eat a bit slower, we've got a source of food there, could sustain our kind for generations.

Lizzie You liar!

Can Those native kids would never want for seafood, ever again.

Lizzie You are such a liar!

Can Glory glory Sophiatown.

Beat.

Lizzie You only said about the strong ones. What happens if the octopus has a weak heart or gets ill, or old.

Can It curls up and dies, I guess. As far as it can curl up. Not having any tentacles.

Lizzie God Themba, you're disgusting.

Can Maybe you're not ready to join our existential brotherhood.

He helps himself to a cigarette.

They didn't nearly kill Sof'town yet. I grew up here, girl, I know these people. They got more tentacles than a very, very healthy octopus. And Mr Drum, he has a warrior's heart, full of poisonous ink.

Lizzie Really.

Can (*CAN remembers something.*) Oh my.

Lizzie What is it?

Can I was supposed to see Henry.

Lizzie He won't mind will he?

Can Na. Henry knows I have the burden of a lover's heart. It's my duty to be always up for love…

Lizzie Is that what this is? Love. Are we playing 'house rules' now?

Beat.

Can House of Truth rules. Always.

She kisses him, his reward for declaring his love. They look at each other for a moment without talking.

Lizzie Canadoce Amitikula von Themba. I love you.

Look at us: Chocolate on cream.

A moment. He rolls her over, gently but decisively, so he is on top. They smile, recognising the symbolism. They kiss passionately. He smiles. She smiles. He starts to slide down the bed, grinning up at her all the way, and she starts to giggle, then squeal like a child being tickled, banging her heels on the bed. Lights begin to fade.

Aggghh! Can can can can can!!

Lights are out.

O God.

7

HENRY, discovered by a spotlight, standing in the street – the same street, and the same part of that street, as scene one.

At some point, as HENRY talks, he fills his pipe. Later, a soft light brings CAN and LIZZIE, lying sleeping on their bed, back into view.

Henry That afternoon I set out to Sof'town looking for Can Themba. I didn't find him. I came three times to the House of Truth, but I still didn't find him; curse that boy's roving ways! So I went to see another reporter friend, Bloke Modisane, and I chatted with Bloke till the early evening. Bloke thought that it was getting late, what with the boys outside getting so knife-happy these days, and urged me to go home early, or to stay for the night. But I explained I had a job to do over in Newclare, and proposed to go and sleep at my cousin Percy Hlubi's house in Western Native Township. So at about 7 o'clock in the evening, I left 'Sunset Boulevard', Bloke's home in Sophiatown – what is it with these guys, calling their shacks by exotic names? – and I went to Western Native, across the rails.

I got to Percy's house about nine, and I explained to Percy and his wife, that I would like to pass the night there. However, I would first like to go to Newclare where I had business to attend. I would return later to sleep. We men sat up talking, whilst Ma Hlubi prepared a bed for me. Before she turned in for the night, she said, 'I'm just thinking, when you get back your cousin and me'll be fast asleep, so don't you knock ja, better you just open the door and go to your bed here.'

Percy looked at the time and noticed that it was close on eleven o'clock. 'Put off your trip to Newclare,' he said, 'It's too late. You can go just as easy tomorrow man'.

'Never put off for tomorrow what you can do today', I back-fired. Then I rose and I walked out into the warm night.

HENRY strikes a match – and lights his pipe. Once lit, he continues.

The next morning, Mrs Hlubi rose early to go to work – she normally took the train at Westbury station.

When she got to the spot where Malatone Street flows out of Ballenden Avenue like a tributary, she noticed a body lying on the green grass, one shoe off, one arm twisted behind, the head pressed hard against the ground, eyes glazed in sightless death.

'Good heavens,' she said. 'Oh my God.'

HENRY casts a glance over at CAN, in bed, asleep.

Can Themba was back home by then, lazing luxuriously, exhausted by his revels. When the news got around he crawled from his bed and staggered over to the spot marked X. There was already a little crowd gathered, and from all the streets flowing into Ballenden people were streaming to the spot.

There it lay in the broiling sun. And all those who stared back at those unseeing eyes agreed on one thing: this was not a good-looking corpse. For the face had been slashed a dozen times. And this chest was a flood of rivers...

Blood appears through his shirt, and down his sleeve, and begins to steal across the space, swallowing CAN and everything in it.

Lights fade; HENRY's life, draining inexorably away.

Blackout.

Interval

8

Lights up on the Drum Office, late afternoon. It is three days later.

The office is a-buzz with action as CASEY, BLOKE, ZEKE, TODD work the phones, type etc.

First CAN, then SYL enter from editor's office. SYL perches on a desk, CAN addresses the room.

Can Okay boys, indaba time. STOP.

CAN's gravitas contrasts with his usual levity. All stop talking, stop typing. Phones are put down, some with a hurried 'Gotta go.' When all are attentive...

It seems we have to get our heads together. Syl, you want to say something?

Syl The headline, as I see it – this is going to be our cover story – Who Killed Mr Drum. Question mark. Photo of Henry. Obituary, to be written by Can Themba. More pix inside.

Casey Not Bob's bulldozer pix then?

Can Bulldozers will have to wait, Casey. Apparently we got a murder mystery on our hands.

Syl Whatever else goes in the issue, Henry is the lead. Henry, and who killed Henry. Perhaps an appeal to the readers. That's all.

Can So. You heard the boss. Casey. What did we get from the Police at Gray's Buildings. They got any kind of clue...?

Casey Still no dice, Can. Zilch.

Can You may need to be a little more specific, Motsisi. They issue a statement, something of that kind?

CASEY consults a flip-pad.

Casey I've got… 'No results from our investigation as of this moment. None expected.' Sergeant… (*Checks his notes.*) …Bezuidenhout.

Can Bezuidenhout, ja. Alright, let's work with that. 'No results from our investigation, none expected.' Todd. Give me something here, something with a twist.

Todd 'None expected.' So er, Is that, No results expected, or no investigation expected.

Can Ja good.

Bloke Al-so, is it the police who expect no results, or the Drum readership has grown used to expecting, 'none expected'? Where our kind are concerned.

Can Kind of convoluted. Leads nowhere. Let's go with Todd. How about we link this with other cases of a similar unsolved nature. Kid?

Casey (*Shrugging.*) It's still a no-score affair, man. From the police side, there's nothing coming out YET. By time we get to press, maybe they've picked someone up. Looks like we're banging the same old Drum, native rag ignores good work done by the city's public servants.

Can 'As of this moment' covers their behinds on this… Zeke?

Zeke Yup?

Can You got anything to add here?

Zeke As a matter of fact, I do. One more brother cut down in Sophiatown. Same place Drum Magazine has romanticised in these very pages…

The others begin to groan – ZEKE's is a familiar tune. In equally familiar fashion, he raises his voice to compensate.

79

…For which the editorial offers to apologise, and while doing that, calls on the native community to bring these bastards to justice.

Can Well, that's a possible angle we could take, Mphahlele, I'm not sure now is the time for mea culpa on this…

Bloke That's right, man…

Todd Why can't the police protect our people, man?

Zeke So what – we rely on the white man's justice? Why can't we demonstrate the power of native self-government?

Bloke Are you saying – it's 'romanticising' when we introduce a little style, a little glamour to the lives of these brothers, is that your 'romanticising'?

Zeke My contention, brother, is we have turned these street gangs into heroes, some kind of film stars, instead of criminals and betrayers of the people, that's romanticising. I'm not afraid to say it; there are people in this room have made a habit, even a reputation on that.

Syl Stick with the story boys, alright? This is about Mr Drum, not us.

(*Prompt.*) Can.

Can Right. So. Who Killed Mr Drum? Casey. Is that all you've got on the police?

Casey It's all I got now.

Can So, may be we think about this another way. Give this a different twist.

What do we think about the police as suspects?

Slightly stunned silence.

Henry had this story running, something he said was called 'Black Velvet'. He talk to anyone else about this? Cops taking advantage of girls they find with paying customers. 'Afrikaaner kops fuck dirty black girls'. You can see they might not want their wives reading that kind of thing. Gives the cops a fair motive to silence Henry, don't you say.

As it registers, CASEY remembers his part...

Casey We got a button too. Police uniform button. Sylvester picked that up from the crime scene on the day...

Button is flipped, and passed around the circle.

Came from off a police uniform.

Todd Stick with it Syl, alright, that's good. But if it is police, that's not so easy. One thing, Henry's face wasn't cut up with no night-stick. We know all about night sticks, it don't cut the skin that way. How does that fit with Henry's murder, where he was cut up with knives so bad?

Casey Yeah, why change the way they usually do it. Kicked to death, back of a kwela-kwela.

Bloke Man, was Bailey ever going to publish this Black Velvet story? You think so Syl?

Syl I don't know. If the evidence was good, I suppose he might. I would have insisted. Yes.

Todd Well, maybe this is what they call a 'special operation' for the police. Nighstick first, then the knife.

Can Zeke? Any ideas on this?

Zeke Me again?

Can We're all working here, right.

Zeke (*Reluctantly taking part.*) We'd have to say, sticking with it, Todd's got it. If it is police cops, the cutting comes after the murder, to make it look like a street killing, covering over the real killer's tracks.

Todd Mmm then again, man, it could be last week, last month, last year – who knows when that button got loose.

Casey True man, while them black police brothers are movin' Henry, maybe one of em' has to stretch across and there's a rub against his shirt-front…piddoing. Henry's already dead when it pings.

Zeke Murder in custody. I like the charge, Can. Wouldn't be the first time. It's a big case to hold together with just a button.

Todd Maybe too big. They'll close Drum down, soon as we print.

Pause. This conclusion is a result for CAN – but he hides it as best he can.

Can (*SYL.*) You wanna say anything on that?

Syl Alright. Let's forget that. Let's push the Police to one side for a moment – what else do we have?

Can OK…the abortionist. Todd. The doctor.

Todd That's right. The Doctor, this abortionist. Henry was followin' up this abortionist story last week. We think, maybe that's what those tsotsis was paid to scare us about. White doctor makes illegal gain out of desperate black girls. Now Bloke can testify Henry came over to his place the day before he died…

Bloke That's right, he was over Sunset Boulevard the whole afternoon –

Can (*Smiling.*) Drinking pin-ups hey?

82

Bloke Drinking champagne, if I might say so brother…

Syl (*Keeping it on track.*) Todd?

Todd The whole afternoon, he was saying he gotta go over to Newclare on some business, like a job, or something.

Bloke That's right. He was real determined about that.

Todd Only first off, he wants to go see Can, for a visit. Can wasn't in.

Beat.

Bloke No, man. He been to Can's before he came to mine. Three times he went over to Canadoce's.

Beat. CAN's turn to push it forward, rather than dwell on the last point.

Can Did he say what business he had in Newclare?

Bloke I don't think so.

Can What? Nothing?

Casey C'mon man, this is Henry. You know his modus. He don't say nothing till he's done it, and then nothing extra till he's got himself a nip of brandy and done the write-up.

Can Alright. So consider for a moment, this backstreet quack's clinic where he practises his deeds, is over there in Newclare, the exact place Henry was headed. That a coincidence, we think?

Casey Henry was going to the clinic? Or coming back, hey?!

Zeke Henry was jumped on his way back from Newclare?

Casey Sure, and this guy followed Henry.

Zeke What guy?

Casey The skebenga, man. The damn tsotsi.

Zeke What tsotsi?

Casey The tsotsi with the fucking knife! The assassin! Or two assassins! Hey, we should use that, Can. Seventy-two point. Henry's Assassins! Wanted by Drum Magazine. Offer some kind of reward…some kind of cash-prize, or somethin'…

Beat. Derisive/bitter laughter at the thought that Drum might offer a reward.

Todd Man, our wages are the only cash-prize round here…

Bloke Yeah and that ain't no reward…

Again, SYL works to keep it on track.

Syl Let's just suppose it wasn't coincidence. That Henry had been to Newclare, to give the clinic the once-over. What then? Zeke?

Zeke None-sense, I'm afraid, Syl. These knife-guys are waiting at the clinic just in case Henry comes by? And when he does come by, they follow Henry right back and jump him when he's almost home? The sort of place people might recognise their neighbour, and fly to his assistance? It doesn't work man.

Casey Why the hang not?

Todd That is the case, Zeke. Nearer to home, farther from the clinic.

Bloke Not his home. Near Hlubi's home. He was going to stay at his cousin Percy's house for the night, the night he was killed. I said that, right?

Zeke Why the hang would they do that? Why not jump Henry at the scene of his crime, his imagined crime from the doctor's point of view, say, if he broke into the doctor's surgery to search for evidence, why not jump him there and then?

Todd We don't know he did break into the clinic. Do we, Casey?

Casey It's not reported by the Police.

Bloke And who's going to report it *to* the Police? Not the doctor if he did cut Henry out.

Todd True, true, if the doctor did do it, he ain't gonna tell the police 'bout the break-in – that would make a connection.

Pause. TODD feels his defeat, throws down his pad.

Cept we don't know there was any break-in. All we got with this abortion thing, is a motive, Syl. There's less evidence here than with this Black Velvet thing. That's it.

Beat. CAN is now toying with his prey.

Can Plus the clinic where the doctor works is not, in matter of fact, over in Newclare. I just threw that in. Keep things moving.

Beat. All are gobsmacked. CAN smiles quickly, and moves on.

Alright. Bloke. Gossip. What's the word in Sophiatown. Who is it the people are saying did for Henry?

Bloke Well, er, you know, there's not too much gossip on the street about this, in actualement Syl.

Can No gossip? In Sof'town? Those bulldozers taking tongues away?

Bloke No man. Sure, I mean…there's the usual loose talk…I'm not sayin' there's no rumours as such…

Can Well come on Bloke, don't spit the boys a curve ball here. Tell us what you heard.

Beat.

Bloke (*Hesitating, clearing his throat.*) There's talk about a girlfriend Henry got. Hometown girl of his.

Zeke You know, this is just what Bloke said it is. Loose talk.

Can I dunno Zeke...

Casey Yeah, we all know, Henry was the undercovers man.

Zeke Hey, you take that back!

Casey I'm just sayin' he was a man of secrets, man, like Todd says, that's all.

Can (*Playing it straight.*) It's true. Henry was a man of secrets. And that would give Henry's missus a motive, if she found out he did have a girl downtown.

Syl (*Losing his rag.*) Jesus. Does anyone here seriously believe it was Florence Nxumalo?

Can Na, Syl's right, Mrs Nxumalo, she's a hard-working nursing sister. If she was going to kill Henry, it would have been poison.

Tension then some stifled laughter at this tasteless, straight-faced joke.

But maybe it was the husband. Or the girlfriend's regular guy. He finds out Henry's been sticking it to his girl, takes out the rival, and that's why he fixes Henry.

Zeke Hey, now I told you have respect for this brother...

Can Or maybe, it was Sylvester here.

Beat.

Todd What?

Can (*To BLOKE.*) You gonna mention that name's on the street?

All attention is on BLOKE – who shifts uneasily.

Bloke What you talking about, man.

Can Syl here wants an investigation, Bloke. It's just a native died, but if we gonna have an investigation, a real life crime exposé, we gotta examine every lead there is. That right, Syl?

Beat.

Syl That's right. Go on Bloke. Let's hear it.

Bloke I didn't hear none of that, boss. I swear.

Can Come on Bloke, stand up straight here. The way we heard it last night, Sylvester Stein done Henry himself.

Todd Hey man, you can't say this…

Syl (*Ending debate.*) Let's hear it, Can. Make it good.

Can Seems Ol' Henry is pushing this lanie editor of ours – I'm just saying the way it is on the street, Syl – he's pushing Mr Stein into doing a big story. Big exposé that's going to make an enemy of the government, maybe lose the baas here his job, get his wife declared a Communist. Kicked out. Could be the Black Velvet thing. Maybe some other story. Syl Stein, he don't want to lose his job, he's got a family and a Buick to think of, he don't want that kind of aggravation. He's just a normal, law-abiding white guy. So he determines to do some aggravating of his own. Or hire some guys to aggravate for him, after the white man's custom. So it transpires, the white boss cuts down his own black workslave, in a story older than time, and the weapon he uses? A weapon so tantalisingly close to his hand every day at his work…a paper knife.

Beat. CAN breaks into a smile – and all laugh, though more with relief than anything

Casey You bastard. It's just Can again Mr Stein, he don't mean nothing.

Bloke Jesus, man, you had my heart pounding-pounding in my chest there!

Todd Man you a bad bad black boy…

Syl Very funny Can, now can we get on…

Zeke You're this brilliant Shakespeare, hey, Can Themba.

Beat.

Can Sure. (*Weary.*) Shakespeare of the Shebeens, that's me. That's what my Bru called me.

Zeke Does this Shakespeare have a plot that works? Or does he just play to the gallery, laughing at us all at the same time. Laughing at Henry, too, while that chum's not even cold in his grave.

Beat.

Can No I have no theory, man. The thing I rest on, as a senior news reporter, is cold facts.

Zeke (*As if to leave.*) The only fact that ever came into this office, was brought in by me or Henry Nxumalo…

Can That's where you're wrong, Ezekiel. 'Who killed Mr Drum?' I don't care for the title, but it tells us one thing. Henry's dead. That hat over there, that's Henry's hat. He was murdered, viciously taken from us. That is the coldest fact I ever heard.

Zeke You need more facts than that to build a case, Canadoce. More than a hat to make you a reporter. The truth is an' no one's saying it, 'cause we loved Henry: Henry was a drinker. Probably he was drunk that night.

He'd never let some bastard jump him otherwise. Police or anyone.

Can You're right, man, we are hiding from facts. Shielding our hearts. But I don't know if the category of facts I consider worthy of our contemplation really interest you. Now if we can all…

Zeke You don't know one fucking fact, Can Themba, not if it wears a name badge and bangs on the door. The only things you respect are fast, and cheap sensations, and you don't mind how they come.

Beat. This is a clear and open challenge.

Syl Steady Zeke. Can's had his joke for the day. Let's hear what his facts are. (*Admonishing the rest.*) Seems no one found too many others, for us to contemplate.

Pause.

Can One. It is a fact Henry was drinking. But we all know Henry, he could drink. I'd go so far as to say, there never was a drinker like Henry in the whole history of Sof'town, and he and I drank with some of the best of those men.

Zeke Sure. But when Henry drank he didn't lose his dignity or his talent.

Can Exactly my point, Zeke. Henry never lost control. Hardly ever. Here's another fact. It was late that night. Bloke here, even Percy Hlubi told Henry, Henry don't go out now, man, leave this business you got till daylight, there are gangs about, thugs to do you harm Henry, stay now. Wait for the safe hours. But Henry – he went out. Out into the night. He crossed the tracks. There was money warm in his pocket that night. Fancy watch on the wrist. But he went alone, to meet his business.

Casey You mean this risk thing again, Henry being a gambler?

Can Not risk, I said already. I don't believe risk came into
it. I believe Henry was a man in control of his destiny.
More in control than any man I know.

Casey Say what?

Beat.

Can As I said, I'm not sure this is the arena for my position
on this. Some other time may be…

Syl If you've got something to say, Canadoce, you'd better
say it. Otherwise, get out my office and come back
civilised. There's work to do. I mean it.

Pause.

Can I have heard, that certain snakes can hypnotize their
victim…

Bloke This doctor done hypnotizing now?

Todd Shush man. Let's hear it out.

Can …hypnotize a rat, a frog or a rabbit, not only so
that it cannot flee to safety in the overwhelming urge
for survival, but so that it is even attracted towards its
destroyer. Almost, it appears to enjoy dancing toward its
doom.

Casey You're crazy, man. You saying it was suicide? Henry
wasn't no bastard self-topper!

Can It's a question my friend. Don't you believe there is
some mesmeric power that Fate employs to engage some
men, deliberately, with macabre relishment, to seek their
destruction, and to plunge into it? See Zeke here, he is
very close to the truth. Only he's too fired up with all his
zealous Africanism to see it.

ZEKE bridles, but is restrained.

Casey It is suicide…!

Can What I'm saying, boys is 'Who killed Mr Drum?' is a simple question. So simple, it is hardly worthy of my answer.

Todd Quit fooling around, man – tell us what you've got or maybe you should shut up…

Can Person who killed Mr Drum? That's the same man who made him. As the book of Genesis says, God breathed man into being. Mr Drum – he's also a creation. He was also brought into being.

Bloke Man, it was Henry invented Mr Drum, him and the old boss, we know that. What you sayin' man?

Casey It's like I said, he says it's suicide.

Can Strike that word from your lips Casey. We all know – our brothers, and our women, die year after year in Sof'town. We kill each other like dogs, tearing at a bone, or we get beaten to death by the police. But you go lookin' for the killer in Sophiatown, it's like the beetle forgot the rock he lives under. My case Todd, and I say this respectfully, is we should forget this foolishness. This 'Who killed…' nonsense. As if we were some kind of gumshoe brotherhood. Some kind of righters of injustice. Give someone else Henry's job. Carry on with our cover girls and our features, until we too reach the point pressed on us from the moment of our birth, till we choose one day not to fight, but to embrace the bulldozer. Welcome the knife. Exhale, that one time too many – breathing out, till the lungs are like the sides of a bag.

Bring down the tent, that the heart may be still. And the lamb feels no pain.

Pause.

Syl (*Ignoring CAN.*) Alright. That's enough. I want everyone out on the street. Anyone you've talked to, talk to them again. Someone knows what happened to Henry. Someone killed Henry, and I want to know why, and how they did it. Let's find them. Now, boys.

Casey He gets to say that?! (*To CAN.*) Man, you been laughing at all of us all this time.

Todd I don't know what he's talking about, man.

Zeke Your hero Can Themba finally drank his brain, Casey. You are talking about the passive submission to white authority! You don't think that's what the supremacists long to hear? Shame on you, Themba! Damn shame!

Todd Zeke come on, out man. Leave it.

Zeke Don't worry man. I don't want to breathe this guy's putrid air a moment longer.

Can I'll see you later, boys. Mr Stein's given me a job to do too. I'm writing Bra-Henry's obituary today.

Syl Out.

They all leave. A beat. SYL and CAN are alone in the room.

My office. Before you go.

Exit SYL to his office, slamming the door. A pause. BOB emerges and is about to slip out, carrying a box under his arm.

Can Hey Bobby. Skipped our indaba again. That way no one knows you just a dumb snapper, hey.

Bob Sure. Whatever you say Can.

Can Do you suppose there's a part of the body more vital than the others? Heart, lungs… Maybe what them liberals say is wrong. Could be it's the skin matters most. Keeps a man apart, and together, stops him spilling all out.

92

Bob This the obituary?

Can Could be. Just as soon as I find some paper.

He searches for some paper in the desk drawers.

Bob Shakespeare of the Shebeens. Henry be proud to have his obituary written by you. You going to put the part about the snake in. The hypnotizing thing.

Can I don't know Bob. Think I should?

Bob I'm just a dumb snapper. I know he was a man of secrets. I think there was parts of Henry no one knew about.

Beat.

Can You too, hey.

What's in the box, Bobby-boy.

Bob Few clothes and things. I've been sleeping back there a few nights, since Gerty Street. Can't sleep, listening out all the time. Going over to my aunt Florence's house for the night, help out. Said I'd keep the kids company, read some stories.

Can Hell, Bob…you're a young man. You oughta live life. When you're done there, come over to my place, doors always open. Door's always open at the…House of –

Bob (*Joining in.*) …at the House of Truth. Henry was coming over to see you, in the afternoon. Before he was killed. That true?

Can That's true. I heard that.

Bob You weren't in, hey.

Can No I was out.

Beat.

Am I your suspect, Bob?

Bob No man…

Can Because between you and me, I have a lady can vouch for my whereabouts all that time. Fact is, I left my trail in some of her more intimate places…

Bob Yeah. I heard that. I almost met the lady. Round at Fatty's.

Can You did. So you coming over? I got a nice bottle of brandy here we can toast your Uncle Henry with. Lizzie could be there too. We can make a night of it if you want to.

Bob No thanks man. I'm gonna stay at Henry's, like I said.

You know they're right about one thing. Zeke and so on. No matter how drunk he got, Henry never hurt people.

Beat.

I'd like to be like him.

BOB exits. CAN sighs, then glances at SYL's door, the light still on. He puts the brandy bottle in his pocket. He opens a drawer, grabs a handful of papers, a book, shoves it into a bag. Going to exit, he pauses by the hatstand, and HENRY's hat. He exits. Lights down, spot remaining on the hat, still in its place, then out.

9

LIZZIE's flat in Westdene. That evening.

CAN and LIZZIE kissing in darkness – not playful this time, but vulnerable, seeking comfort. They kiss, pull back a little, smile, kiss again.

LIZZIE pulls away and switches on a bedside light.

The floor is dotted with balls of discarded paper. Also on the bed, a typewriter, and two bricks, or bits of rubble.

Lizzie Why did you bring them up here? The bricks?

Can I don't know. Something this cop said. Henry was hit on the head then stabbed. 'The way they do it in the bush.'

Lizzie Is it true?

Can I don't know. I've never been in the bush.

They laugh gently. LIZZIE picks her moment. CAN pours a drink.

Lizzie I may have to leave, Can.

Can This friend of yours needs her flat back, hey. We'll find somewhere.

Lizzie Not the flat.

Beat.

Dolly's going, did you hear?

Can Dolly? Now Dolly I can believe. Toddy-boy and his musical masterplan. Escape in the chord of G.

Lizzie She's excited. London I think. West End.

You'd love London. You're always going on about Victor Hugo, Dickens, London is Sophiatown, with… pavements.

Can (*Joining in.*) …with pavements.

Beat. LIZZIE tries again.

Lizzie Nobody gives a damn in London, what you are…

Can (*Overruling.*) Rooms vacant; blacks dogs and Irish need not apply.

Beat.

Lizzie It's not impossible, that's the point. You could come to England. We could live freely.

Can Would you be there, if I was there. In London?

Lizzie Yes.

Can House of Truth, hey Lizzie.

Lizzie I don't want to live in any other house. Do you?

Pause.

Will Sylvester take you back again? Again, again?

Can Never come between the bossman and his houseboy. Ours is a long, long, war of attrition.

Lizzie He did want you to be editor after him.

Can We both know that's not going to happen. Drum magazine holds a mirror to Sophiatown. White owner, white editor, native staff.

Lizzie You're the favoured son. If you weren't he'd have sacked you long ago. That's what you told me.

They're going too. Sylvester and Jennie.

CAN evades, smiling.

Can Where do you get all this information, Liz-girl? You'd make a darned good reporter, my dear.

Lizzie You should know by now. White people read each other, women gossip. Lovers lie and deceive…or tell the truth and suffer.

Can And I must live in the House of Truth forever.

LIZZIE picks up a screwed-up piece of paper, and unfolds it.

Lizzie Some of these you didn't even write on.

Can The Shakespeare of the Shebeens was lacking the necessary lubrication. (*Raising his glass, thanking her.*) Guzundheit.

Lizzie You can find something good to say about him can't you. He was your friend. Everyone liked Henry, even you. He was a hero.

Can Of course, but you know, heroism is a choice. There must be a choice for the act that follows to possess true merit. Did Henry choose to be Mr Drum, or did Mr Drum choose Henry for his own carnivorous ends.

Lizzie You should come to London. While you can.

Can This is that suffering you were talking about.

Lizzie It's not your fault Can, you were just out.

Can I KNOW IT'S NOT MY DAMN FAULT!

Beat. LIZZIE starts to clear away the paper.

Lizzie I was worried when you didn't turn up, that's all.

Can Worried?

Lizzie You weren't there. The Back o'the Moon after work. Look at me, I'm turning into a bloody housewife.

She spills the paper.

Can The dear old Back o'the Moon. Dangerous to go there on your own young lady.

Lizzie Casey was there. He looked after me. He was in quite a state. Beside himself.

CAN pours more drink.

Can Casey. He's a good friend to have in a corner.

Lizzie You're persona non-grata now, is that it? They're shunning you.

Can I don't know, who are 'they'?

Lizzie Something in the way they were with each other. Bloke and him. No bickering. Like they'd lost their elastic.

97

Can There was a small difference in opinion concerning the interpretation of recent occurrences in the neighbourhood and the onward trajectory of the estimable organ that we serve.

Lizzie (*Pursuing.*) As if they're in pain. Henry was their friend too, Can.

Can You want me to stay now or go?

Lizzie People in Westdene gossip too, I can't… I'm scared, alright.

Can You had a visit from the police?

Lizzie No.

Can They called you in?

Lizzie Would I be here if they had?

I have to go Can. I have to leave soon.

Can You know, if the government is tired of your company girl, you know about it.

Lizzie That's not the way it works is it. Not on my side of the line. Word gets passed along. Friends of friends. Information is delivered. The way you find a new shebeen.

Can (*Sudden temper.*) Jesus, this is just…there is no place for me in London! There is no reason for me to leave this place.

Lizzie Well there's me. Isn't that a reason?

Can And Mr Hutchinson? How will he feel, me walking arm and arm with his wife, looking him in the eye as an equal. Saying fuck off basie-mine, I'm fucking your missis.

Lizzie I wouldn't be his missis. I'd be your missis.

Beat.

Can No no no no. You are going to him.

Lizzie I can't be in prison, you can't ask that of children. If I'm deported I'll never get back in. I'll never see you again. Can think about that; I'll never hold you again.

Can So er what, wait a minute. The Nats give me an exit visa, a one way ticket, and they never let me back in? What is that? Is that love, Liz-girl? Is that carry my bags boy, yes missis, what is that exactly, do you think?

Lizzie That's not my fault.

Can Not your fault.

Lizzie The first time we met, at Jim Bailey's place…

Can Ja, I know what I said.

Lizzie 'We outnumber you five to one. Each of us could kill one of you and there'll still be enough of us to govern. Before we begin, you'd better remember that.' Quite a line to lay on a girl, I thought.

Can I think you'll find the genius was in the 'before we begin'.

Lizzie You were telling yourself. It's not a private thing between two people, not just love between two people, not here. They won't let it be. I have to go away from you, or away with you, or 'we' puts me in gaol. You in gaol. If you're lucky. Or you'll end up like Henry.

Can You know, there are worse things than being like Henry. He was a hero, everyone liked Henry.

Lizzie Drunk all the time. So drunk you look sober. Mysterious just to have something to own, that's yours. Do you think you are so different from Henry? Henry was just further round the dial, that's what happens to people. Good people, lovely people. They get crushed.

The life we're living – we can't live it. It means you're alive, a human, they can't have that. The House of Truth is going to be rubble, Can. Just rubble.

Beat.

Can Well, that's alright Liz-girl. We belong to the dust, we are drawers of water, hewers of wood…

Lizzie Live in the House of Truth, Can, please.

Pause.

I have to go.

Can Yes, yes, quite. I'll come, Lizzie. London, New York, Paris, wherever my dear. Where you go, I go…

Lizzie I'm going to bed.

Can YOU ARE NOT GOING TO DAMN BED!!!!!

Pause.

Lizzie I don't feel safe anymore.

She exits. CAN is left looking into the abyss.

Lights fade.

10

The street, where HENRY died. Night. A dog barks off.

CAN enters. He stares drunkenly at the ground.

Can (*Shouting.*) Henry…!?

He grabs at a handful of dusty soil and lets it run through his fingers.

No fucking blood.

He drinks from a brandy bottle. He tips the last of it onto the ground.

Gezundheit, Captain.

He spins round and smashes the bottle against the wall. The dog's barking increases in response – though still distant.

Come on, sportsman. Best sportsman in the whole ffffffffucking universe!! Why not me? Why not fucking Casey, for Christsake…

He reaches into his pocket – another bottle. He smiles again.

Gezundheit.

He drinks. And pours HENRY another one. Off, a truck approaches and pulls up. CAN peers down at the ground.

Nope. No blood.

CAN looks in the direction of the truck, but makes no effort to escape. The squeak of a truck door. Dogs bark – near at hand now. The door slams. CAN raises the bottle to toast HENRY again.

Gezundheit!

He throws the bottle over his head, and the wall behind him. He speaks to the approaching cops, showing his hands are empty.

No hands, man.

He is picked out in the harsh flare of a searchlight beam. He attempts to shield his eyes. Barking of dogs is now close and threatening, the dogs straining at their leash. Two black cops enter – MOETSIE, and another KOP.

Bez (*Off.*) Stop there! You forgot the curfew, kaffir.

Can Yes basie, I forgot, I'm a silly fucking kaffir, my basie…

Bez (*Off.*) You're a stupid blerry schwartze! Too blerry careless, ja?

Can Very very careless, my Basie…very…

CAN peers into the darkness beyond the bright light – and makes out a face he recognises.

Hey, Sergeant… Sergeant Bez…Bez…

Kop Bezuidenhout!

Can Sergeant Bezuidenhout, that you? Hey man, it's me! (*To the kop nearest.*) Why the pale face, boetie? It's ol' Bezuidenhout.

A smaller, sharper beam picks out CAN's smiling face.

Bez (*Off.*) Ag, shut the dogs up. Shut them up! I know this kaffir.

BEZ enters on stage, carrying his torch.

Naturelle Themba. Lost your basie, ja? What are you doing here?

(*To the kops.*) Assistant Editor Drum Magazine! Look at this kaffir. Look what a shitpile you can make. Better you make a polisie for a career. Give yourself some dignity, ja?

Kops (*Laughing obediently.*) Ja, basie.

Can (*To the kop.*) Shitpile… He's a reader, hey.

Moetsie Nag Pass!

Can …always good to meet a reader. S'alright man. The baas knows me.

Moetsie Pass jong!

Bez Dark as a cunt these nights. Think you blerry invisible. You Drum boys should learn the dangers of the district.

Beat. There's a threat in this that registers with CAN.

Can It's here, baas. Some damn place… Aw Shit…

CAN pulls out his pass…along with a couple of playing cards. The KOP goes to pick them up.

Bez Leave it. Give me the pass.

Black KOP glances at the passbook, passes it to BEZ.

Moetsie Hier's hy, baas. The pass.

Bez (*Inspecting the pass.*) You were at a card game, Naturelle.

Can No man…it's just…you're right, basie. My Bru died, baas. Right here. I was…there's no fucking blood here, Bez.

Bez Drink taken, and gambling. And immorality. Consorting in the district, with a racially forbidden female. That's what I'm hearing.

Can No baas, not me.

Beat.

She's leaving basie.

Bez Ag the meisie is leaving him!

Can Everyone's leaving. I…came for a drink. Conversation… Little Sartre with my Bra Henry.

Bez Un-educated naytiffs. I have no problem with these people. (*He means his cops.*) How can we raise the kaffir with this example?

Moetsie, come to me.

Moetsie Baas?

Bez Give me the stick in my hand. Quickly.

Moetsie (*Nervously; they've played this game before perhaps.*) You have it baas.

The stick passed over, the kops starts to move away…

Bez Wait! Move when I told you, ja?

Moetsie Sorry baas. Baie dankie, baas.

MOETSIE steps back, and stands stock still. BEZ walks around him. Moetsie is clearly afraid of being struck, but daren't move.

Bez One beating. All it takes for that good, uneducated kaffir to learn.

No good for you, hey. You are a shit kaffir. Veilgoed. Vrot. Go home and quickly, Naturelle. While you still have a house. Dankie Moetsie.

He passes the stick back to MOETSIE.

No more favours for this kaffir. You see him again in this street, after curfew, you beat him hard. Donner that ou. Hard as hell. You hear?

Kops Yes baas. We will baas.

Bez Ja. (*To CAN.*) You see. I don't want you in my station. You go straight to hell.

Exit BEZ.

Can Hey, what's wrong with me now, man.

The black cop shakes his head and sucks his teeth, hefting the stick in his hand, relishing the prospect of beating CAN. Dogs bark again, loud and threatening. CAN talks to the kops, a different tone now BEZ has withdrawn.

That's the game, hey boys? I walk away, the dogs follow? That's how it is for me? Hey?

Bez (*Off.*) Back in the truck boys! Quickly now!

Moetsie Wozani Madoda! Kwelani!

The KOPS walk away – a tide going out, leaving CAN stranded.

Oda.

Can What's wrong with me now? Bezuidenhout!

Engines start up, competing with the dogs straining at their leashes.

What the fuck is wrong with me!!!

Trucks move off. Distant dogs bark. CAN falls to his knees, completely broken, as lights fade.

11

LIZZIE's flat in Westdene. Night.

LIZZIE is packing. She has been drinking, and is in equal parts erratic and upset, throwing things into the case, rather than packing. A knock on the door – three knocks.

Lizzie Go to hell!

Again, three knocks. LIZZIE throws the empty brandy bottle at the door, where it smashes. She goes back to her packing.

A third set of three knocks. LIZZIE's voice is low, defiant, wiping back tears.

It's open you stupid fuck.

The door opens.

Enter DOLLY – in an expensive looking coat. She could be talking about the welcome, or the flat. Either way, She is fairly sarcastic.

Dolly Nice.

LIZZIE is genuinely surprised, both that it is not who she was expecting, and to see DOLLY in unfamiliar circumstances.

Lizzie Dolly? What are you doing here?

Dolly Do you have a candle Mrs Hutchinson?

Lizzie What? Yes. Of course I have. Why?

Dolly Please, fetch me the candle and a match. Quickly.

LIZZIE exits. DOLLY takes the opportunity to scan the suitcase and/or an empty bottle. When she returns, LIZZIE has recovered her assertiveness.

No need to ask what you've been doing tonight.

Lizzie You haven't come all this way to sneer, Dolly. Or to borrow a candle. What do you really want?

Dolly Please, light the candle and put it in the window.

Lizzie Look, why don't you tell me...

Dolly Why don't you do what the black woman says.

Beat.

Lizzie Perhaps, it's because you've just walked into my house in the middle of the night...

Dolly Your house, my country. Who's the guest? Give the candle to me..

Lizzie No. It's alright. I'll do it. If you just told me what's happening like a normal adult we wouldn't be arguing.

LIZZIE can't strike a match – too shaken up, and shaky. DOLLY softens a tad.

Dolly Here. Let me.

DOLLY lights the candle and puts it on the windowsill.

There.

Lizzie This is about Can.

Dolly Turn off the light.

LIZZIE obeys. A moment.

Lizzie Now I can't see. Has it occurred to you I don't want him back. When he does come home he's drunk. He's a bastard.

Dolly We've all felt that way. With Can you don't have a choice. Like I don't have a choice when my friend's lying in the street, with his head broken from a bar-fight.

Lizzie Is he hurt? O God is it bad?

Dolly It must be nice, knowing if it gets hard you can leave.

Lizzie What if I don't want to leave. What if I want to stay.

Dolly Then you're insane. Or stupid. Or in love. Obviously you're packing so you're none of those. Drunk. O yes. I forgot that.

LIZZIE stands to peer out of the window.

Lizzie What's happening. Who are you signalling to?

Dolly Sit! I show up less.

DOLLY's turn to look out of the window.

Don't worry. He won't be coming up here.

Lizzie Can won't?

Dolly My friend. My other friend. (*With some satisfaction.*) He doesn't trust lanie women. He thinks they can't be bought. Of course you can, you're just more expensive. They are always likely to let you down. That is a lesson every darkie has to learn. In the end, you just can't trust a white.

Lizzie If you're talking about me…

Dolly Ssssh.

They listen. Off a car door slams.

107

I heard it said, you can guess how rich a man is by how many steps he lives from the street. You have got a lot of steps. But not enough. Your 'little heaven' here's over. Can needs you.

Lizzie Thank you, I think I know that. That it's over, I mean.

Dolly You told him?

Lizzie I tried.

Her eyes adjusted to the dark, LIZZIE carries on packing. DOLLY sits on the bed.

Dolly Poor Canadoce. He's always talking. Talk talk talk talk. Talk so much talk he don't have to listen. Can used to be my man – he tell you that?

Lizzie (*Quickly.*) Yes, yes he did.

Dolly I never understood most of his talk. Used to grunt now and then, that was enough for a while. Course I don't have your education.

Lizzie That's his territory. That's where he has control. The only thing he's any bloody good at.

Dolly (*Arch.*) That's not quite how I remember it.

Lizzie I told him there was a choice. Either we leave, or I do. He seems to think if he stays, so will Sof'town. We can just carry on as we are. It's pathetic. Childish.

Dolly Did you see that wall downtown, Victoria Road? WE WON'T MOVE. Big shiny letters. Hell it's easy when you don't have a choice. When you get a choice, it always gets messy.

She smiles, and strokes her coat.

Me, I like nice things. But they have to be paid for, I learned that one. These Drum boys…Bloke Modisane, he loves champagne – do you ever go to Bloke's house?

Lizzie Once.

Dolly 'Sunset Boulevard'! A suit-smart man serving canapés, in a shack leaning on his mother's house. All the time bulldozers come and go, the neighbours disappear, china rattles – and all Bloke drinks is champagne. From an egg-cup, of course. Zeke's got his studying, turning himself into a damn situation. Casey's got his bottle, Todd's got his music – and the bottle. Who wouldn't drink champagne if they had the choice? And who wouldn't rather believe they had a choice, even when they don't.

Lizzie Is that what happened with you and Henry, you had no choice?

Dolly What's that?

Lizzie They say Henry had a girlfriend.

Dolly Girl, if I had a pound every time some man claimed I was his girlfriend, God knows, I wouldn't be singing for my supper. Henry Nxumalo was my friend.

Lizzie I'm just telling you the rumour. Some people wonder if it was the girlfriend's man killed Henry.

Beat. DOLLY approaches LIZZIE – and slaps her across the face.

Dolly You better sober up, ja!

Pause.

Hang, I didn't mean to do that. You've got enough trouble.

Just as DOLLY goes to try to comfort LIZZIE the door is kicked open, TODD enters, struggling with the slumpen, bloody form of CAN. TODD dumps him without ceremony on the bed. He straightens himself up, and nods at LIZZIE.

Todd How do you do, Mrs Hutchinson?

Lizzie Fine, thank you.

All are unsettled, looking at the body.

Dolly Soon you can go, if that's what you need. I'll send someone to fetch him. Two knocks, a break, then a third. That's the signal. Till then, get him in some kind of shape. He'll be better away from the shebeens. Come on Todd, we don't want to keep my friend waiting.

Lizzie Wait, you can't just leave him here. They could be watching the house.

Dolly Who? Who's watching?

Lizzie Someone pushed a note through. Security Police. I think they must be watching. Special Branch. They say I'll be deported if I stay here.

Todd We should go, Dolly.

Dolly Maybe I'll see you in London, Lizzie. Your country, my house. My theatre, ja. We'll drink champagne. Talk about the good old days in Sof'town.

DOLLY exits. Beat. TODD steps forward, offering a handshake.

Todd Goodnight, Mrs Hutchinson. Parties always end with a broken head.

LIZZIE accepts the handshake.

Exit TODD. LIZZIE looks at the body. She seems almost stunned, unable to move – or maybe just like the rabbit before the snake, she is entranced. Lights.

12

LIZZIE's flat, a week later. Morning. CAN is sitting on a chair, positioned so he can see out of the window, but cannot be easily spotted through it. He is eating soup from a bowl.

Nearby, a suitcase.

LIZZIE enters. She has been out shopping. She shows little sign of the distress and anxiety of the previous scene. In fact, she is positively chirpy.

Lizzie How's the soup?

Can Thank you my dear, it is very good.

Lizzie I make good soup. And I buy marvellous presents.

She leans over to kiss him – a bright peck. CAN is clearly still stiff – though not exactly the English Patient. This was the latest in a long line of batterings, rather than a brush with death. LIZZIE takes off her gloves and leaves them on the bed. CAN refers to the kiss.

Can That was the present?

Lizzie (*Taking out record.*) No. I went to Ah Sings in town. Want to hear it?

Can You've been to Sof'town?

Lizzie Only to buy records. Ready for this?

Can Yes, missis.

Lizzie You have to dance.

Can With my ribs?

Lizzie Of course. Think of me as a priest. You have to be declared clean so you can return to your people.

They are dancing.

Can Maybe I want to stay dirty.

Lizzie The opposite to clean is unclean. If you're unclean, they give you a bell and you stay an outcast for ever. Tough.

Can How is this?

Lizzie Not bad.

Can Am I clean yet?

Lizzie Quite clean.

Can I get a drink?

Lizzie No, you have to stay clean.

Can You see any of the Drum boys? Todd, Casey?

Lizzie No. I wasn't looking. You've stopped.

Can I like to look. I watch you, and I feel the strength flooding back in again.

Lizzie That wasn't the treatment.

Can I'm trying not to get too dirty. Hey, you hurt your face there?

A knock on the door distracts them – two knocks; a pause, then a third.

Lizzie Sylvester was on the step. I asked him to wait a while. He probably has to get back to the office.

Can Hang Lizzie, I don't… (want to see him)

She goes to answer the door. SYL enters, in addition to his own hat, he carries another, and a bag of fruit.

Hoozit, Syl.

Syl Dolly asked me to come by. I thought I'd…Oranges.

He puts the bag of fruit down. Beat.

112

Lizzie I'm going out to get a few things. Leave you guys to talk.

She picks up the case.

Goodbye Can.

LIZZIE kisses CAN – it could have been a lingering one, but it wounds them both too deeply, CAN especially. She picks up her coat. Exit LIZZIE. A pause. CAN moves to the window, and watches her go. Pause.

Can What are you doing here? She asked you to come?

Syl No. No, it was Dolly really. I would have come before but Lizzie wanted to give you time to recover. I did say I'd give her a ride to the airport.

Can I am not going to apologise.

Syl No. No, it's me that needs to apologise. I made an error, Can.

Can An error.

Syl About Henry.

Can Well, Henry don't mind, Syl. He's dead now. Everyone knows, he is very very dead now.

Syl I can be a bit of a blerry boy-scout, I know that. Things in order, nice and neat. The way I was brought up…

Can Hey, Syl…

Syl I'm not just talking about Africa time. Henry getting killed, that's the worst hangover ever. All you want is something to take the edge off. I wanted us to put pressure on the police. Get them to check a few facts, find things out. But there's hardly a law at all for you people. All you can do is change the question, like you were telling us if I understood it right.

But we have to do something.

Can Shit man.

Syl Nobody writes like Can Themba, Todd's going, we have to get this thing moving, fast now.

Can Man. You say there is no law for us, but you still believe you can do something. What will you do Syl? Question suspects? Establish a motive? I cannot walk freely down a street of my choosing. I cannot drink a glass of alcohol, I can't sit down on the nearest park bench to steady myself, I can't even love the woman I love – the Law says that's not allowed. Do you think the law is going to recognise Henry's killer? Even if the killer is under his nose? Henry Nxumalo was not supposed to be an adult when he was alive. He was a boy, he was plain Jim, he was perpetually an infant, you think the law's going to call him a man now he died?

Syl So what, we just give up? Listen Can, we owe Henry.

Can I don't owe Henry a damn thing.

Syl Jeezuz Themba, don't do this...

Can You know, Henry used to bring his eldest to the shebeen sometimes, she would be eight, nine years old – she'd sit outside while her daddy got a skinful. That was Henry too, Syl. He was living his life – good, bad, a lot of bad – but he was a free spirit. Then along comes Mr Drum. Holds a mirror to the world.

We used to have this thing we said. Henry and me. Lucky Narcissus. 'Lucky Narcissus, Bru. When he looks in the pool, in a mirror, all he sees is beauty. What does a slave see?'

If it was not for Drum Magazine, Henry would still be at the dogtrack. Florence Nxumalo would not have buried a husband who was only at home one night in ten, and that little girl would still have a daddy. Who killed Mr

Drum? Man, Sylvester. Maybe you should ask what
Drum Magazine was doing that night.

Pause.

Syl Maybe you're right. But that was Henry's choice…

Can There is no choice! You can be a child, or you can be
a punchbag, that's it! And I know I'm right, I don't need
you to tell me.

Pause. SYL throws his hat on the bed.

Syl You're not a bohemian, Canadoce. Jesus. Children?

Can Really? An' I thought that was my problem. My
bohemian lifestyle. Bloke Modisane with an education,
the same unlikely aspirations to a literary life.

Syl Except yours aren't unlikely, are they.

Beat.

Alright, look, I understand. Your life is your opposition.
The way people should be free to live…

Can Don't. Don't change my life into something
meaningful. My life is nothing but meaninglessness and
futility and it is rendered so by the insanity of white
fucking people.

Pause. SYL flops on the bed.

Syl So you think being a lanie makes you meaningful?

Toe the line or get out. That's how bloody meaningful I
am.

Can So what. Are you saying you're not getting out?

Syl White boy jumps ship. Nothing new there, hey. Except,
this is my country too, God help me. And you guys
– you and Henry, Todd, Bloke, even Casey, you're the
best of it.

Pause. SYL, somehow finds fresh energy to stand.

Anyway, we're not talking about an investigation anymore. That stunt we planned. At the church. That's what we're going to do. Mr Drum walks again.

Can That is just as bad man. Reacting and reacting...

Syl No no, I don't think so. That's the beauty of the idea. Time the white buggers reacted for a change. We force them to react, just by planting a black backside on a pew. Right there, in the middle of Afrikaner land. I'm not pretending there won't be a beating involved, somewhere along the line. But we know you've taken those before...

Can What?

Syl Don't laugh, alright. We tried once already. Twice. With Bloke.

Can You let Bloke be Mr Drum?

Syl Bloke chose the Methodists. Those folks liked him so much they wouldn't let him go. Made him stay for tea after. No pictures there for Bob, hey.

CAN can't help but smile. A moment.

So. This time it's going to be the Nats. Your Dutch Reformed Church, down the road here. Could get tasty. Bloke's not so keen this time, obviously. He seems to think he's done his bit. And that leaves you.

Pause.

I want us to do something Can. I want us to pull something off. You know why.

Can Swansong. So Sylvester can leave his benighted land, all self-respecting. Esteemed by the native.

Syl I was thinking of something else. A friend of ours, who didn't get much of a choice.

He takes out a roll of notes.

Contents of the expenses (account). Get yourself a new suit, Themba. Or buy a ticket to England, if that's what you have to do. Go after Lizzie. For godsake don't drink it. I'll come by tomorrow. If you're still here, sober, we'll talk about the stunt, plan it out.

SYL stops by the door.

You know, if it was the government killed Henry – I've no idea if it was or it wasn't – if it was intended as a message, it worked. I don't think Jim Bailey dares scratch his arse these days.

Exit SYL. A moment. CAN unhurriedly walks to the window, glancing out. He turns back in, picks up LIZZIE's gloves and holds them to his nose, while looking at the cash, lying on the bed.

13

Street. Morning.

Lights up on ZEKE, TODD, BOB, BLOKE and CASEY squatting against the side wall of a church. BOB is at the stage right end of the wall, on look out.

Above and around them, church bells begin to ring.

Todd Jeez, man, do they have to ring those damn bells so loud.

Everyone tells him to shush.

Casey Rough night, heh Matshikiza.

They laugh.

Bob Hey – Here's Syl.

SYL strolls into view – smartly dressed, hat in place, confidently upright in contrast to his cowering/hiding staff. Once past the end of the wall, he pulls in close, so he won't be seen.

Syl Morning boys. How's it look?

Bloke Hey, Syl, I ain't doing this man. I told you, au contraire for me on this one, I said that.

Syl Its OK Bloke, you won't have to.

Bloke There's no one else, man. There's no one!

Syl Calm down, man. Alright? Can will be here.

Bloke What?

Zeke Canadoce? Are you sure about that?

Syl I am sure. Can's been on a bit of a jag, boys, that's all. He's…definitely going to be here.

SYL's anxious glance around undermines his words – and the general confidence.

OK? So – Casey, got the plan?

Casey (*Doubtful.*) Sure, man.

Syl Well?

Casey If Can does show – I mean, if we do get a Mr Drum today – Syl here goes into the church nice and early, gets a good seat.

(*To SYL.*) Bob's got a camera for you. Keep it under your jacket. When they all stand up to sing the first hymn, that's the signal…

Todd (*Looking off.*) Gee and Shucks, man, I seen me a vision!!

Enter CAN.

Can Morning boys, hope you don't mind me joining in worship today…

Pause – the gang are not quite sure how to react to the prodigal's return. BLOKE produces a silk handkerchief, breaking the tension, and tucks it into CAN's breast pocket

Bloke You know, I always said Can would make a terrific Mr Drum!

Terrific to see you, Bru!

Can Thanks Bloke. Hey Casey. How's it going Kid.

Casey (*Full up.*) Good, Can. Good to see you, man.

He nods to, and gets a nod from, ZEKE and BOB.

Can Boys. So, we ready to go, Syl?

Syl Soon. Casey was giving us the low-down…

Casey Like I said – Syl here goes in the church. We wait till them good boers of Westdene are all standing for the first hymn…

Bloke Be careful man. You even step in there, those Afrikaners are going to come down on you like a ton of porkmeat.

Todd That's it, Bru, you got it!

Bob Yeah, We have got to have pictures, man. Brutality.

Casey Relax man, we don't have to worry about Can no more. He lives with Lizzie now. He practically is a lanie.

They all laugh – though not CAN and SYL, who exchange a glance.

Syl Alright. I'll have the camera inside the church. Bob here…

Zeke Yeah we got it Syl. To my mind, should be a bomb you take in with you, not a camera…

He is shushed – as much to silence the sentiment as the noise of his voice.

Can We set now?

Casey (*Checking watch.*) Soon. Alright – the hymn starts, Can goes in. If the white folks are standing up, they won't all see him straight away – means Mr Drum can get a seat before anyone tries to rush him. Bob man, you have to work fast, get the action while they throw him down the church steps.

Bob Sure thing, man.

Syl On that point boys – the story has to have pictures. Bob has to get away, or his camera. There's a kwela-kwela parked round the corner too. That's where you come in.

Zeke Diversion? For the police? Or do we get arrested?

Syl Work as runners; scatter, or run as a team. Whatever looks like it'll work, just get the film back safe.

Casey Time. You better go Syl.

Syl I'll meet you back at the office, or maybe Fatty's. Good luck, boys.

Casey Go man!

Syl (*To CAN.*) See you in church, Mr Drum. Here. I brought this.

He passes HENRY's hat to CAN. SYL exits. Pause.

Casey Anyone take thirty?

Bloke What, seconds?

Casey I don't mean minutes, man.

Todd Yeah, I'll take it. Maybe these white folks ain't so bad on a Sunday.

Casey You got it. Me, I'm on twenty-five seconds. They're bad all week round. You in Can?

Can No no, I think I'm going to be out, pretty damn fast. I'll take ten seconds.

Bob Take longer than that, march you outa there. Put me down for thirty five-seconds, man.

Laughs, jeers, cries of 'What?'.

Can Man, thirty-five seconds? You think I'm gonna get down the front of the damn church…!

Zeke Length of time before an Afrikaner's racial intolerance kicks in? Five seconds gets my vote.

Equal jeers.

Casey Hell man, he gotta have gelignite power, get out that fast.

Todd You know Can, man, he's always loaded…

Casey So, ladies and gentlemen, all done at that?

Bloke I'm in for twenty seconds, Kid. Kinda, middle of the aisle position…

Casey You got it, Debonaire.

Bob OK, Syl's in the church door boys. Cops not moving. Looks good. You ready Can?

Can Sure. We talking a fiver on this, yeah?

Casey Why not.

Can Ten if my nose gets broke, you hear?

A few wry smiles – this could indeed get nasty.

Todd Want a drop of some extra courage, Can? Take the edge off?

TODD offers CAN a swig from his hip flask.

Can No, thanks, man. I'm keeping a clean head today.

General but controlled amazement at this.

OK. One, for Henry.

Todd For Henry man.

The bottle is passed all the way round.

Can Henry had some nerve, do this stuff all the time, hey boys.

Casey You be fine, Can.

Can Hell I know that. Just a face like mine, got more to lose than Henry's ever did…

They laugh. Church organ – which may have been tinkling away, suddenly vamps up – the first hymn.

Casey That's your cue, man. They going ta sing at us now. Go to it.

Can I looking smart enough to you?

Bloke Not bad, man. Pretty deb-on-aire.

CAN nods and exits, as they clap him on the back.

Casey You now Bob.

Bob Sure.

Casey Who's got the watch?

Todd I got it. He inside yet?

Bob Not yet… Alright, start the watch! I'm gone boys.

BOB goes to exit – and is picked out with a spot.

Todd (*Out.*) Bob Gosani, got the job at Drum through his uncle, Henry Nxumalo. One of the greatest snappers Drum ever had. Young Bob only lived a few more years after Henry died – double pneumonia, the doctors said. Most say a broken heart.

(*Looks at watch.*) Five seconds. You lost your money, Zeke.

Ditto.

Zeke Todd Matshikiza. Jazz writer, musician and composer of South Africa's greatest musical, *King Kong*, about a black boxer who won't lie down. When the crackdown came, Todd got out alive. His career failed in England though, and Todd was homesick. Died a musician's death, still exiled, in Zambia.

BOB reappears, leaning on the stage right edge of the wall.

Bob Unlike Zeke Mphahlele. He got through one university degree after another on them correspondence courses, teaching all the while to support his interlectual habit. Zeke is still alive, 'bout the only one who is, teaching, and writing in the new South Africa. Keeping out of the shebeens helped Zeke become one of the country's greatest writers.

BOB goes again.

Todd Ten seconds, that's your money gone Can Themba my friend.

Who's next?

Bloke I got twenty!

Casey William Bloke Debonaire Modisane. Wrote all Drum's social stuff. Lived with his mother in this decrepit yard in Sophiatown, complete with refrigerator, wind-up gramophone and dainty snacks and cocktails he served to his 'visitors'. Escaped to England with ambitions to be an actor – then wrote an autobiography called *Blame Me on History*, in which I get one, measly, mention...

Todd You lost your money, too Bloke.

Casey So, it's just you and me now, Matshikiza!

Bloke Casey Motsisi. Not much to say about that short little man. Disciple of Can Themba. He died too; of a alcohol-related disease – it wasn't always Cola in those bottles – but not before he achieved fame in Jo'burg for his regular Drum column called A Bug's Life – in his version, a biting satire on apartheid...

Dolly Bloke Modisane – You gonna mention the ladies at all tonight?

DOLLY has entered stage left.

All Dolly!!!!!!!!!!!!!!

LIZZIE enters stage right.

Lizzie Dolly Rathebe speaks for herself. Love girl. Cover girl. African beauty, singer and one-time film star. Lost her place in the musical – but they loved her at home. Still singing, till 2004, when she died, aged 74.

Dolly One-time film star?? Who is that talking?

All Advise us Dolly!!

Dolly Lizzie Hutchinson. Not her real name. Pale-skinned English beauty. Came back home to England, Can Themba's heart in her hands. Broke. Still living in London, that Sophiatown with pavements.

Casey Hey, quiet, somethin's happening now boys....

DOLLY and LIZZIE exit. Organ music collapses...

Hear that?! O man. They seen his black face now alright!!

Todd Twenty five whole seconds!!!!!!!!!!!!!! Hey man, I won it all myself!!!

Bloke The hell you did! He said they got be out of the church. Mr Drum just turned a few heads so far – Shit. Casey wins.

Todd Casey?

CASEY has taken over as look-out.

Casey Here comes our Mr Drum, boys… Ouch! Man that's gotta hurt!

Stop the watch!! Jesus, Bob!!! Get it on film, man!!

Police sirens. Shouts off, whistles.

Todd Shucks man. All he had to do was take a seat near the back, I'd a had a win there!

Zeke (*Laughing.*) Here come the kwela-kwelas…

Off, shouts.

Casey (*Watching, flinching.*) Ow! Man, that's painful! (*He looks again.*) Fuck! He's comin' our way!

Bloke Police?

Casey Can Themba!

Zeke Shit!

CAN enters, at pace, looking fairly beaten up, breathless.

Can Go boys, they comin' fast!!

Casey We need the camera, man!!!

BOB arrives, holding out his camera. It gets thrown like a hot potato.

Bob Go go go go go!

Todd I don't want it!

Zeke Nor me!

Bloke No no no! This shirt's my best one!

Can Go Casey! Go on, man! Go!

Beat.

Casey Alright. Stay close boys!!!

CASEY exits stage left. No one else moves.

Can Get out of here!

Exit ZEKE, TODD, BLOKE.

You too, Bob, get out of here. Go on, I'll be fine.

Bob Sure?

CAN nods. Exit BOB. CAN has clearly taken a couple of blows, and is hurt. Enter SYL, also looking roughed up.

Syl You alright?

Can Great! They gone back to their praying yet?

Syl I don't think so...I think they lost their religion.

They lean against the wall, winded, laughing... Enter HENRY, wearing his hat, of course.

Henry Sylvester Stein. White-boy editor of the Bantu paper, Drum. Left for England just after the bulldozers came to Sof'town. Soon as Jim Bailey started censoring his magazine. Worked as a newspaper man all his life, then frittered away his retirement writing some damn-fool book or other.

Can *(Slapping SYL on the shoulder.)* You damn kaffirboetie, Syl. Kaffirboetie!

Henry And Canodoce Amitikula von Themba. Intellectual disciple of Sartre. One of the great hopes of Black South Africa. Never was made editor. Sacked, in fact, by the man who came after Syl: 'Unreliable'. Took a job as a high school teacher in a girl's college far, far from Jo'burg. Drank, and drank some more and like the others, died young. Was drink the cause of his death? Well, I know where it started…

Syl Sure you're OK?

Can No man. (*Only half joking.*) It's killing me.

SYL and CAN – having caught their breath – exit. HENRY lights his pipe.

Henry Which leaves Mr Drum himself. The original Mr Drum, Henry Nxumalo. Well. You all know what happened to Henry.

There was a story, many years later, that a prisoner stalked by the shade of Henry Nxumalo, confessed the murder was on his conscience. He said there was an arrangement with a man named Lefty who paid him £120 for the job. Exactly who Lefty was acting for, no one knows, but the going rate for murder in the townships at the time was only £25. Speculation said it must be a lanie footed the bill – who else pays over the odds that way?

£120, for the head of Mr Drum. Do you think they overpaid?

He squats, picking up two small rocks, in echo of scene one.

Who killed Mr Drum? Who crushed that circle of fine young skulls? Maybe it wasn't a person at all, or not just a person.

He bangs the rocks together.

Or maybe it was no one. Because Mr Drum, he never died.

He tosses them down again.

Apartheid's swept clean away now just like they cleared Sophiatown. We even got a black President. But, you know, not everything has changed...

Dolly (*Off, calling.*) O Henry...

Henry But you don't want me ta bore you with no earthly talk.

DOLLY appears at the side.

Dolly You comin' to bed now Henry?

Henry Do you know in the afterlife, everyone gets a Dolly Rathebe, all to hisself?

He smiles, as township music kicks in. HENRY turns to exit. Lights.

The End